A NEW APPROACH TO
CAPITAL BUDGETING
FOR CITY AND COUNTY GOVERNMENTS,
SECOND EDITION

Richard F. Wacht
Professor of Finance
Georgia State University

HJ
9147
.W33
1987
West

Research Monograph No. 87

1987

A15040 285275

Business Publishing Division
College of Business Administration
Georgia State University
Atlanta, Georgia

Arizona State Univ. West Campus Library

Library of Congress Cataloging-in-Publication Data

Wacht, Richard F.
   A new approach to capital budgeting for city and county governments / Richard F. Wacht. — 2nd ed.
      p. cm. — (Research monograph / College of Business Administration, Georgia State University ; no. 87)
   ISBN-0-88406-190-6
   1. Capital budget—United States—Mathematical models. 2. Local budgets—United States—Mathematical models. 3. Capital investments—United States—Mathematical models. I. Title. II. Series: Research monograph (Georgia State University. College of Business Administration) ; no. 87.
HJ9147.W33   1987
352.1'2—dc19   87-21157
                                                              CIP

Published by
Business Publishing Division
College of Business Administration
Georgia State University
University Plaza
Atlanta, Georgia 30303-3093
Telephone: 404/651-4253

Published 1980. Second edition, 1987.
©1980, 1987

All rights reserved, including the right to reproduce this publication, or portions thereof, in any form without prior permission from the publisher.

91   90   89   88   87   5   4   3   2   1

Georgia State University, a unit of the University System of Georgia, is an equal educational opportunity institution and an equal opportunity/affirmative action employer.

Printed in the United States of America

Book design by Marcia L. Lampe

Cover design by Patton H. McGinley, Jr.

Phototypesetting by Donald E. Dedmon

CONTENTS

Preface vii

Acknowledgments ix

CHAPTER 1 AN INTRODUCTION TO CAPITAL EXPENDITURE MANAGEMENT 1
    Importance of Capital Expenditure Analysis 2
    Administering the Capital Expenditure Budget 4
        Generating Projects 4
        Project Evaluation 5
        Expenditure and Budgetary Controls 6
    Financial Viability: The Decision Criterion 7
        The Problem of Intertemporal Comparisons 8
    The New Approach 9
    Summary 10
    Appendix to Chapter 1 11

CHAPTER 2 THE CAPITAL BUDGET PLANNING MODEL 17
    Initial Capital Investment 18
    Net Operating Revenues (Deficits) 20
    External Financing Requirements 21
        Noncapital Funds 22
        Property Tax Increases 23

Revenue Bonds	24
General Obligation Bonds	25
Combinations of Financing Options and Programs	26
Financing Temporary Deficits	27
Summary	28

CHAPTER 3 AN ILLUSTRATIVE APPLICATION OF THE MODEL — 31

Voluntary Donations	34
Property Tax Increase	35
General Obligation Bonds	41
Revenue Bonds	44
Summary of the Data	47

CHAPTER 4 OTHER FEATURES OF THE MODEL — 49

Project Timing	50
Rising Project Costs	50
Falling Project Costs	52
Cost Minimization	54
Uncertainty	54
Budgetary Controls	58
Aid to Cash Management	60
Summary	61

CHAPTER 5 A CAPITAL BUDGET MODEL FOR SMALL CITY AND COUNTY GOVERNMENTS — 63

Part 1. Program Description	68
Part 2. Inflation and Interest Rate Adjustments	76
Part 3. Financial Viability Tests	83
Section A. Gifts and Grants Option	84
Section B. Tax Increase Option	89
Section C. Revenue Bond Option	93
Section D. General Obligation Bond Option	99
Part 4. Project Cash-Flow Characteristics	106
Part 5. Project Controls	111

CHAPTER 6 A COMPUTER-ASSISTED VERSION OF THE PLANNING MODEL   **119**
  Input Format   **120**
  Computer Output   **128**
    Gifts and Grants   **133**
    Tax Increase Option   **136**
    Revenue Bond Option   **137**
    General Obligation Bond Option   **141**
    Supporting Calculations   **147**
  Summary   **147**

To my
Mother and Father
for their
love and support

Preface

This second edition of *Capital Budgeting for City and County Governments* had to wait until I caught up with the data-processing revolution brought about by the increasing popularity and use of microcomputers in business applications. The model presented here is basically the same as that contained in the first edition, published in 1980; however, in this edition the computer support required to generate quick and accurate solutions to capital budgeting problems has been updated. Instead of requiring a mini- or mainframe computer, the model now runs on a microcomputer.

As did the first edition, this book presents a definitive treatment of a method designed to assist city and county governments with the tasks they face in planning new capital investment projects and long-lived, noncapital programs. The approach to planning presented here will help decision makers to insure that all the relevant financial data are considered before a project is accepted and implemented. When projects are properly planned, they also can be properly financed and, consequently, stand a better chance of being successful over time.

The complexity of the model will be evident from examining the chapters leading up to the illustrative examples. These chapters, while clearly "academic," permit insight into the structure of the model for those decision makers who are comfortable dealing with abstract mathematical presentations of decision methodologies. For these individuals, the effort required to understand the way in which the model works will pay dividends by allowing them to modify and extend the model to fit the particular needs of their municipalities.

The accounting/budgeting approach, used to illustrate the model in the first edition, has been retained. Its presence in this edition serves two purposes. First, it provides a clear illustration of the model in the accounting language that all managers and decision makers understand, regardless of their levels of education and experience. And second, for those city and county governments that may not yet use a microcomputer, the budget manual format can be readily adopted and put to use in their planning processes.

The final chapter of this book presents a kind of user manual for the microcomputer-assisted version of the planning model. This version of the model runs on the Lotus 1-2-3™ spreadsheet software. (Lotus 1-2-3 is a trademark of Lotus Development Corporation.) It is completely interactive; that is, the user merely enters data in accordance with instructions given by the computer. The model then takes over and does the calculations and prints out the results on command. The template is contained on a 5¼" floppy disk and is available from the Business Publishing Division of Georgia State University at extra cost.

Acknowledgments

I happily acknowledge the help and support provided by the Business Publishing Division in bringing out this second edition. In particular, my thanks goes to R. Cary Bynum, director; Margaret F. Stanley, editing supervisor; and Claudia Forman, assistant editor, for their tireless efforts and endless patience in bringing this edition to press.

Dr. Clayton B. Doss, research associate with the Center for Public and Urban Research at Georgia State University, played a major role in encouraging me to apply the model's basic concept to planning in the context of city and county governments. He continues to provide support for my research and instructional effort in this area, and for this I am most grateful.

The computer-assisted version of the model is the exclusive work of Sheila D. Frazier, Southern Engineering Company, who worked nights and weekends to create the Lotus 1-2-3 template. As a result of her efforts, many city and county planners may be able to avoid working nights and weekends on their capital budgeting problems.

While I owe these individuals a debt of gratitude for their contributions to this book, I must bear final responsibility for its quality. I am therefore culpable for all errors that may remain herein.

CHAPTER 1

AN INTRODUCTION TO CAPITAL EXPENDITURE MANAGEMENT

This chapter begins the task of describing a new approach to capital budgeting for municipal governments by examining the importance of capital expenditure analysis, the administrative process involved, and the criterion on which municipal capital expenditure decisions should be based. A brief introduction to the model on which this new approach is based concludes the chapter.

The terms "capital expenditures" and "investments" usually refer to the commitment of resources made with the expectation of realizing future benefits over a reasonably long period. For present purposes, this definition will be broadened to include both the *acquisition of real assets*—such as buildings, roads, and water systems—and the *creation of long-term programs*, such as fire safety inspection programs or summer employment opportunities for teenagers.

The use of the broader definition of capital expenditures is justified because both kinds of investments exert an almost identical impact on the long-range financial health of the municipality making the investment. Both alter the cash receipts and disbursements patterns of the spending unit for an extended period and both should be subject to long-run analysis before funds are committed. Thus, the acquisition of real assets or the commitment of funds to a noncapital-based program must be planned for, implemented, and controlled with equal care to prevent either of them from precipitating future financial problems for the municipality. (The terms "municipal" and "municipality" refer to both counties and cities, as well as to their agencies and to any authorities they may have created. The term "spending unit" carries the identical definition.)

Importance of Capital Expenditure Analysis

The nature of the investment in fixed assets and long-lived noncapital programs requires an approach to planning that is both more formal and more analytical than that taken in planning for any other kind of purchase that a municipality normally will make. There are several reasons for this.

First, the consequences of investments in capital projects extend far into the future. The decision to acquire fixed assets or create new programs, therefore, influences the patterns of cash flows into and through a municipality, both immediately and for longer periods than almost any other kind of spending decision. For example, a decision to construct a solid waste disposal system will permanently alter the character of a municipality's organization—its operations, cash flows, and financial structure—as new management and employees are hired, operation and maintenance costs are incurred, and revenues are collected.

Second, capital expenditures often are irreversible, except

at considerable financial and managerial cost to the spending unit. Since the markets for many kinds of used equipment are either thin or nonexistent, the only alternative to continuing to use a recently acquired but undesirable asset is to scrap it and start anew. Starting anew, of course, means an added financial burden to the municipality or a loss of its cash reserves. It also may mean that the municipality's managers must spend more money to retrain employees to operate new equipment, must deal with the problems associated with an interruption of services during installation of the new equipment, and must expend the many extra hours needed to attend to the almost inexhaustible list of details that accompany the start-up of a new facility.

Third, if the municipality is to experience growth, its government must recognize that the desired growth can take place only if it is willing to make a series of investment decisions involving fixed assets and long-term programs. Further, if a government wishes to avoid financial stress while a municipality grows, the investment decisions have to be made on sound bases. Otherwise, the governance of the municipality will be characterized by *crises* management in which the majority of managerial time is spent in "firefighting" with little remaining for planning and control.

Finally, the impact that any particular capital investment project has on the financial wealth of a community depends on many internal and external factors. The relationships among these factors are at best complex; consequently, the decision process itself must be complex in order to encompass as many of these factors and their interrelationships as possible. For example, the costs of supporting any new program are *future* costs, and the future is never known with certainty. Cost inflation can quickly make budgetary appropriations for operating and maintenance costs (which often are approved six months to a year in advance of the actual expenditure) completely inadequate to support a particular program at its planned scale of operations. Thus, any approach to capital expenditure planning must be *long range*, must explicitly consider the effects of *price level changes*, and must encompass as many of the other factors as are likely to influence the cash receipts and expenditures of a proposed capital expenditure project. The ways in which these factors are handled in the decision process comprise the essence of the analytical approach presented in this book.

Administering the Capital Expenditure Budget

Budgeting for capital expenditures is an administrative as well as financial process. Although this book deals primarily with decision making, the search for new projects, the evaluation and implementation of projects selected, and the exercise of continuing control over the entire process are equally as important as the decision itself. The decision, which must encompass the financial and economic aspects of capital expenditure analysis, is only the starting point. The larger and more difficult part of the process is its administration, which begins after the decision is made and continues on a daily basis throughout the life of the project.

Generating Projects

The need for a long-range community or county development plan ought to be self-evident. The implementation of that plan within a growing municipality should produce a continuing and growing series of capital projects. The relatively lower quality of life tolerated by many community and county residents, when compared with others in similar circumstances, may result from the failure on the part of government either to develop a long-range plan or to properly implement its plan by generating a sufficient number of capital projects that are consonant with the municipality's long-run objectives.

While many capital budgeting projects simply "appear"

without much effort being expended by government officials in searching them out, such projects are often deficient in some respect. And the resulting list of projects may comprise a haphazard patchwork of proposals leading in no particular direction, when considered within the context of the municipality's long-range plan.

This is not to say that proposals that merely happen along should be discarded without examination. No proposal should be rejected or accepted without benefit of careful analysis. But the municipality should not depend solely on the spontaneous generation of a stream of new proposals to supply all of the investment alternatives for the capital expenditure budget. Instead, it should attempt to insure a steady flow of projects by adopting a systematic approach to capital expenditure management, starting with integrating the search for projects with its long-range planning efforts.

Project Evaluation

The government official specifically charged with the management of the financial affairs of the municipality—let's call him or her the fiscal officer—plays the role of "project analyst" in the capital expenditure process. He or she is responsible for two types of project evaluation. The first deals with subjective matters that determine whether or not the project is acceptable from the point of view of *municipal goal achievement* or *cost-benefit analysis*. Any proposed capital project must pass this hurdle before it can be considered a candidate for further serious consideration by the municipality's decision-making authority.[1]

The second type of evaluation—that with which this book is mainly concerned—is the critical *financial* evaluation of the project. Specifically, the fiscal officer must evaluate each project's relevant cash flows to determine whether or not the project is (or can be made) *financially viable*. The data on which this determination is based are generally provided by engineering, economic, and demographic analyses, and to some extent, by current financial and economic indices obtained from readily available sources (e.g., the *Wall Street Journal* and the municipality's bank of deposit).

While the results of project evaluation are of great importance, the final decision concerning each proposal is not always based on these criteria alone. When competently performed by the fiscal officer and completely understood by the decision-making body, however, project evaluation can significantly influence the final decisions. For example, the second type of evaluation can clearly indicate which projects are likely to contribute to the financial stability of the municipality and which are likely to cause financial distress. And because the decision makers are responsible to their constituencies, they cannot often afford to overlook the quantitative aspects of project evaluation.

Expenditure and Budgetary Controls

Funds appropriated for projects selected during the evaluation phase make up the *capital budget*. Two types of controls are necessary to insure that the time and effort expended on generating and evaluating the projects are not wasted and that the funds allocated to various projects will provide maximum benefit to the municipality.

Expenditure Controls. The first type, *expenditure controls*, insures that funds are spent as they were intended to be; appropriations become budget figures for each project in the capital budget, and actual expeditures, as evidenced by invoices and employee time cards, are charged against the respective project's budget. Most municipalities add 15% of the total construction or acquisition cost of the project to cover engineering and design costs and to allow for contingencies.

Budgetary Controls. The second type of control, *budgetary controls*, is concerned with operating cash inflows and outflows on a project basis and serves as a check on the project evaluation and selection processes. Such controls are ordinarily left in place for at least several years after the project's completion, and preferably over most of the project's life.

The budgetary control system compares actual cash flows with those originally forecasted. This kind of comparison enables the fiscal officer to monitor actual performance and prevent it from diverging too far from forecasted operations before corrective action is initiated. If corrective action is not taken in a timely manner, severe and chronic financial stress can occur, the origins of which may not be readily discernible. And unless a project that is known to be financially *nonviable* (or that has subsequently become so) is adopted on the strength of its nonmonetary (subjective) benefits, it should not be permitted to continue in operation, no matter how large an investment was initially required. The admonition against "throwing good money after bad" is an excellent guide in these circumstances.

Financial Viability: The Decision Criterion

As mentioned earlier, the fiscal officer must evaluate each project to determine whether it is (or can be made) *financially viable*. Since the major portion of this book is devoted to examining and explaining how to plan for and measure financial viability, a complete definition of this concept is in order.

As a first approximation, financial viability means preplanned, financial independence expressed in incremental cash-flow terms on a project or program basis. In other words, a capital expenditure project can be considered financially viable if the fiscal officer can identify (and have earmarked) a sufficient amount of cash (1) on hand, (2) in the form of expected future cash inflows, or (3) both on hand and coming in to completely cover all of the current and future cash outflows associated with that project. Future cash *inflows* include borrowed money, tax receipts specifically assigned to the project, and operating revenues received from the sale of the project's output of goods or services. Cash *outflows* include both the initial outlay for capital assets (if any) and the recurring cash expenditures for normal operations, maintenance, and debt service over the expected life of the project (or some other extended planning period).

The viability criterion also requires that systematic or predictable changes in the project's cash flows be fully accounted for in the evaluation process. The effects of inflation, changes in the tax assessment caused by municipal growth or changes in property values, and the interest expense and income associated with borrowing and investing surplus cash must therefore be explicitly recognized in measuring project financial viability.

The rationale for applying this criterion to capital expenditure analysis is simply that all new projects or programs should be planned to achieve their desired results without diminishing the resources allocated to or the benefits being provided by other new or ongoing programs. The successful application of this criterion, therefore, will show the municipality how to keep from "robbing Peter to pay Paul" insofar as capital spending is concerned.

The Problem of Intertemporal Comparisons

Since the viability criterion requires the fiscal officer to examine the project's relevant cash flows over time, he or she must be able to compare on a common basis the sums of money received and paid out at different times. This is necessary because money has a "time value." That is, a dollar received today is more valuable than a dollar to be received with certainty a year from now, because money in hand can be invested and earn interest. Cash that will not be received until later does not have that earning ability; hence, differences in "time values" of money must be accounted for in long-range planning.

The problem of adjusting cash flows to a common base has two dimensions in the context of the viability criterion. The first relates to the need to consider the effects of *inflation* on future cash flows. This dimension is expressed in terms of *compound sums* or *future values*. The second relates to comparing all future cash flows with today's cash on hand. This dimension is expressed in terms of *discounted sums* or *present values*. These two dimensions are presented and discussed briefly in the appendix to this chapter. Since these concepts are of fundamental importance in later chapters, the reader who may not be familiar with them is encouraged to carefully examine that material.

The New Approach

Briefly, the approach to municipal capital expenditure evaluation—or capital budgeting—described in detail in the following chapters enables the municipality to test new programs for financial viability. The method involves comparing cash outflows for construction, equipment purchases, and operating costs with the cash inflows from any one or a combination of several financing options, including debt financing, grants or other contributed funds, tax revenues, and operating revenues.

The approach employs the concept of the time value of money in equating the present value of future cash outflows with the present value of future cash inflows from the relevant financing options, both of which are adjusted for the effects of inflation. When the cash inflows and outflows are equal, the project is exactly viable. When they are not equal, the approach clearly indicates both the reason why they are not equal and the steps needed to correct the condition. For example, when cash inflows exceed the outflows, the municipality may elect to increase the scale of the project or reduce the amount of external funding originally planned. The results of the calculations will indicate the maximum size of the project and/or the maximum amount of money needed to make the project exactly viable. The same kinds of indicators are provided when the program is underfunded; that is, when cash outflows exceed inflows.

In addition to producing an estimate of the program's funding requirements, the approach permits the municipal fiscal officer to find the answers to "what if" questions. For example, the engineering report may specify operating costs at a certain level. The fiscal officer may ask, "*What if* these costs are 10% higher? How will that affect the program's financing costs?" By changing the cost estimates to allow for uncertainties surrounding the estimates of future cash inflows, the fiscal officer can measure the impact of the estimates on the program's viability.

The approach also allows the direct entry of operationally or politically determined restrictions on tax increases, bond issue size, and other variables. It provides cash-flow data that is usable as a basis for establishing post-decision control systems for expenditures and operations. Finally, it may be applied either manually (i.e., with the aid of a hand-held calculator) or run on a microcomputer in a spreadsheet format.

Summary

A system of capital expenditure management is important to all city and county governments because (1) the political and economic impacts of investments in capital projects extend far into the future; (2) decisions to invest are often irreversible; (3) such decisions significantly influence a municipality's ability to grow and prosper.

The measurement of relevant cash flows and their evaluation for decision purposes make up only one phase of the entire capital expenditure process. The process itself begins with a systematic search for new projects, continues through the evaluation and decision phase, and concludes with the creation and implementation of controls. The entire process focuses on achieving financial viability for all new programs. This goal insures that the municipality will avoid future financial stress as a result of decisions to undertake new projects.

Endnote

1. Unfortunately, this type of evaluation is beyond the scope of this book; however, a rather extensive body of literature dealing with cost-benefit analysis is readily available. A potentially more useful framework for qualitative analysis of investment projects is found in Richard F. Wacht, *Financial Management in Nonprofit Organizations* (Atlanta: Business Publishing Division, Georgia State University, 1984), 373-392.

APPENDIX TO CHAPTER 1
The Concept of the Time Value of Money

Compound interest plays an important role in almost all financial decisions, including, of course, the determination of project financial viability. It permits the decision maker to compare on a common basis dollars paid out and received at different times. That kind of comparison is essential because a dollar in hand today does not have the same value as a dollar to be received at some distant future date. And that is the result of the opportunity to invest dollars in real or financial assets that earn *interest* (or a profit over and above the cost of the asset). In the simplest case, if a person has a dollar today, he or she can lend it at some rate of interest and receive more than a dollar in return at the end of a year. Interest is therefore the price at which money is exchanged for a promise to pay at some future date. And interest is what gives money a *time value* and what causes the timing of cash flows to take on importance in financial decisions.

Future Value

The basic formula for calculating simple interest is

$$I = Prt$$

where I = dollar amount of interest to be received
 P = principal sum invested or loaned
 r = interest rate, expressed as a decimal
 t = time, generally in years

If a person has $3 to lend, requires a 10% interest return, and schedules a one-year maturity on the loan, at the end of the year he or she will receive $3 plus interest amounting to

$$I = \$3 \times .10 \times 1 = \$0.30$$

The total amount to be received at the end of the year is therefore $3.30. This amount is the *future value* of $3.00 on hand today, at 10% interest for one year. If we abbreviate future value as V, we may express this concept algebraically as

$$V = P(1 + r)$$

If the borrower in the preceding example wished to use the money for two years and wanted to make payment of principal and interest in full at the end of the second year, he would have to pay interest at a *compound rate*. That means he is paying interest in the second year on the interest accrued during the first year. Thus, the amount to be paid when the debt matures in two years (i.e., the *compound sum*, or future value) is

$$\begin{aligned} V &= P(1+r)(1+r) \\ &= P(1+r)^2 \\ &= \$3(1+.10)^2 = \$3(1.10)^2 \\ &= \$3(1.21) = \$3.63 \end{aligned}$$

For periods longer than one year, the general formula for the compound sum becomes

$$V_t = P(1 + r)^t$$

where $t =$ the number of years being considered.

The quantity $(1 + r)^t$ can be thought of as a number called a *compound interest factor* (or *CIF*). Tables containing compound interest factors for different combinations of values for r and t are presented at the end of Chapter 5. Table A, for example, lists the *CIF* for 6% interest at nine years as 1.6895. Thus, if you wished to calculate the future value of $100 at 6% for nine years, you would locate the *CIF* in the table and multiply it by $100 to determine the future value of the principal amount of $100, which is, of course, $168.95. Relatively inexpensive hand-held calculators with pre-programmed compound interest capabilities are available and are fairly easy to use. These devices simplify the calculations by permitting the user to enter the principal, interest rate, and number of compounding periods to produce the compound sum with only a few key strokes. Regardless of how the calculations are performed, the formula for the *CIF* is inherent to the process.

Present Value

In many cases, the amount to be received on a future date is already known, but its *present value* or *discounted sum* is unknown and must be calculated. Zero-coupon bonds, for example, are sold at a discount from the amounts at which they will be redeemed at maturity. The difference between this "discounted purchase price" and the redemption value of a particular bond will determine the yield or interest return the buyer will receive from his or her investment in the bond. The lower the purchase price of the bond, the higher will be the investor's return.

The relationship between the present value and future value of any financial asset is expressed in mathematical terms as a reciprocal. In other words, if P_o is the present value (and purchase price) of a zero-coupon bond, and V_t is its known future maturity value,

$$P = \frac{V_t}{(1+r)^t} = V_t \cdot \frac{1}{(1+r)^t}$$

Suppose an investor decided to purchase a zero-coupon bond provided she could obtain an 8% return on her investment. What price should she offer for a $10,000 bond that will mature in one year? The answer is

$$\begin{aligned}P_o &= \$10,000 \cdot \frac{1}{(1+.08)^1} \\ &= \$10,000 \times 0.925926 \\ &= \$9,259.26\end{aligned}$$

The fraction $1/(1+r)^t$ can be thought of as a number called a present value factor (*PVF*). Table C at the end of Chapter 5 contains present value factors for different combinations of r and t.

Annuity

The *CIF* and *PVF* are useful only for finding the value of cash promised at one future date. When a *stream of equal payments* continues for a number of years (an annuity), these factors cannot conveniently be used to determine their future or present values. Instead, a special set of *CIF* and *PVF* are used, and these are found in Tables B and D, respectively, at the end of Chapter 5. The method of calculating the future and present values remains the same; the only difference is that they represent the values of a *stream* of equal annual payments for given periods and given interest rates.

Quarterly and Monthly Compounding

Thus far, we have examined cases in which interest was compounded on an annual basis. In most instances, however, interest is paid or charged quarterly, monthly, and sometimes daily, and compounded on the same basis.

The conversion from annual to more frequent compounding is simple. The formulas and method of calculation remain the same, but r is divided by the number of compounding periods in one year and t is multiplied by the same number. For example, suppose the investor in the preceding example required a yearly return of 8% *compounded quarterly*. In this case, r would become $(.08/4 =) .02$, and t would equal $(1 \times 4 =) 4$, and

$$P_o = \$10,000 \cdot \frac{1}{(1 + .02)^4}$$
$$= \$10,000 \times 0.923845$$
$$= \$9,238.45$$

The lower purchase price that results in this instance indicates that more frequent compounding periods produce more interest for the investor, because interest paid in earlier periods earns additional interest in subsequent periods. In the present example, the investor's dollar return increases by $20.81 as a result of quarterly, rather than annual, compounding.

Monthly compounding works in an almost identical way. Continuing the present example with monthly compounding, we find that r becomes $(.08/12 =) .00667$, t is $(1 \times 12 =) 12$, and the purchase price of the bond is equal to $9,233.61.

Applications

The *CIF* will be used in this book to adjust cash flows for inflation and growth. The *PVF* will be used to compare all cash flows on a common base—their present values. The *PVF* of an annuity will be used to determine the annual payments needed to retire a bond issue of a certain size and to discount certain equal annual cash flows, such as debt service charges and operating costs and revenues.

CHAPTER 2

THE CAPITAL BUDGET PLANNING MODEL

This chapter presents the capital budget planning model in rigorous mathematical terms to reveal as clearly as possible the interrelationships among all of the factors included in the planning and decision process. This presentation of the model shows how the model works and thus permits the user to make modifications to better suit any special circumstances encountered during its application. For most readers, however, a once-over-lightly reading of this chapter will be sufficient to capture the essence of the model's construction. The abstract notions presented here are repeated in a much more concrete and vastly more interesting and readable form in Chapter 3, where the model is applied to a hypothetical, yet realistic, example. Chapter 5 presents the model in yet a more basic form—a capital budget manual in the familiar accounting format.

Cash flows associated with a municipal capital expenditure program can be separated into three parts. The first is the initial capital investment required to build and equip the facility (or simply establish a noncapital-based program) and prepare it for operation. The second part consists of the program's *net* operating revenues (or deficits), and the third part is the external cash inflows needed to insure its financial viability.

The third part is unique to this model. In other contexts, the external financing requirement generally is set equal to the initial capital investment and treated as the dollar amount to be financed in one way or another. The financial viability objective imposed by the application of this model, however, requires that *all* cash flows be examined over the expected life of the program. When program revenues and operating and maintenance costs are brought into the picture, external cash requirements can be less than, equal to, or greater than the program's initial capital investment. Similarly, for programs not requiring an initial investment, some external financing may be required.

Initial Capital Investment

Equation (1) is used to calculate PVI, the present value of the program's inflation-adjusted, initial capital investment.

$$PVI = PVB + PVE \qquad (1)$$

where *PVB* is the present value of construction costs and *PVE* is the present value of equipment costs, both adjusted for individually applicable inflation rates and discounted at r, the return on investment of the municipality's surplus cash or its contingency reserve fund. While maintenance of the model's symmetry requires that the discount rate also be adjusted for the effects of inflation, such an adjustment would introduce burdensome complexities into the exposition. For example, the discount rate, r, may be properly defined as

$$r = i + p + E\left[(P_1 - P_o)/P_o\right] + f(m) + e$$

where i is the basic interest rate for the class of securities purchased, p is a risk premium, $E[(P_1 - P_0)/P_0]$ is the expected inflation effect, $f(m)$ is the term structure effect, and e is an error term. Since municipalities generally are limited by law to a list of "approved" investments of a riskless kind, p may be assumed to be equal to zero. We may also assume, without doing great violence to the truth, a constant average maturity of securities held in the reserve fund and an inflation effect equal to zero. Hence, r may be treated as a known constant.

Since project cash surpluses and deficits generally pass through the contingency reserve fund, the rate of return represents both an explicit return and an opportunity cost to a municipal project; hence, r is the relevant discount rate. The cost of capital for the municipality is irrelevant since the objective of this model is to break even on a cash flow basis and not to achieve wealth maximization (see note 1 in Chapter 1).

The present value of construction costs is defined as

$$PVB = \sum_{t=n}^{m} \left[B_t(1+r)^{-t}(1+i_B)^{n-1} \right] \quad (n = 1, 2, \ldots, m-1) \quad (2)$$

where n and m are the years in which construction begins and ends, respectively, B_t is the construction progress payment made at the end of year t (based on the contract price of building the facility beginning in $t = n = 1$), and i_B is the annual inflation rate applicable to construction costs. Since construction estimates usually include allowances for cost inflation over the contract period, the adjustment for inflation, $(1 + i_B)^{n-1}$, relates only to the year in which construction begins (i.e., $t = n$). In other words, if $n = 1$, $(1 + i_B)^{n-1} = 1$, and no inflation adjustment is required. If construction is scheduled to begin in $n = 1$ but is delayed one year, construction costs will increase by $(1 + i_B)^{2-1}$. The longer the delay after a bid is accepted, the more costly will be the facility (in nominal, or unadjusted, terms).

Equipment costs, including donor relations and dedicatory expenditures (where applicable), generally are incurred at the end of the construction period, or in year m. The present value of these costs is

$$PVE = [E(1 + m)^{-m}](1 + i_E)^m \tag{3}$$

where E is the total equipment cost, and i_E is the appropriate inflation rate for equipment. If the expenditure on E encompasses more than one year, PVE becomes the sum of the present values over the relevant period.

Net Operating Revenues (Deficits)

Net operating revenues, NR, are defined as total revenues generated by the program (exclusive of tax revenues) less incremental cash operating costs. Overhead cost allocations, depreciation, and financing costs are excluded from this definition, since they are accounted for elsewhere. For any given year, the project may produce revenues, break even, or incur operating deficits.

Net operating revenues generally begin in the year after construction is complete (i.e., in $t = j$) and continue to year k. The present value of this cash flow is

$$PVNR = PVR - PVOC \tag{4}$$

where R is the current estimate of the project-generated revenues and OC is the project's estimated operating and maintenance costs. Both of these variables are expressed in current, nominal dollars. Equation (4) can be restated as

$$PVNR = \sum_{t=j}^{k} \left([R_t(1+i_r)^t - OC_t(1+i_{oc})^t] (1+r)^{-t} \right) \quad (5)$$

where R_t is the expected revenue in year t, OC_t is the expected operating and maintenance (O and M) costs in year t, and i_R and i_{oc} are the inflation rates applicable to project revenues and O and M costs, respectively. Further refinement of this equation, as well as equations (2) and (3), is advisable when the components of construction, equipment, and O and M costs are subject to significantly different inflation rates. For example, historical inflation rates for paper were about one-half of that for fuels during the period 1979–85. Thus, decomposing the cost variables may provide better estimates of future cash flows.

External Financing Requirements

The external financing required to achieve financial viability for a new municipal program generally is available from at least one of four basic sources: (1) noncapital funds, such as grants, gifts, or community fund-raising campaigns; (2) a property tax increase; (3) revenue bonds; and (4) general obligation bonds. The test for financial viability—given legal, policy, operational, or political limits on external fund-raising—involves selecting one of the four financing options and then comparing total funds available with the program's cash requirements on a present-value basis. Since the precise form of the test depends on the option selected, the test for the individual options are examined in the following sections.

Noncapital Funds

Most noncapital sources of funds involve both immediate cash inflows and commitments by the grantor to future installments over one or more years. The nominal value of cash receipts net of collection costs, Q, is calculated as shown in equations (6) and (6a).

$$PVQ = PVI - PVNR \qquad (6)$$

$$PVQ = Q\left[b_g(1+r)^{-1} + \sum_{t=1}^{2} \frac{b_2}{2}(1+r)^{-t} + \right.$$

$$\left. \sum_{t=1}^{3} \frac{b_3}{3}(1+r)^{-t} + \ldots + \sum_{t=1}^{a} \frac{b_a}{a}(1+r)^{-t}\right] \qquad (6a)$$

where b_g is the percentage of Q received as one-time, first-year cash inflows, and b_2, b_3, ..., b_a are the percentages of Q to be received in equal annual installments from pledges of 2, 3, ..., a year's duration, respectively. The terms within the brackets in equation (6a) reduce to a present-value factor, f, which, when divided into PVQ, yields the nominal dollar amount, Q, required to achieve program financial viability solely out of noncapital sources of funds. Thus,

$$Q = PVQ/f \qquad (7)$$

If Q is too large relative to what a municipality anticipates it can raise from grants, gifts, or other similar sources (i.e., if $Q > Q_{max}$), the program fails the test of financial viability.

The alternatives for handling financially nonviable programs are discussed later.

Property Tax Increase

Property tax rate increases generally are limited by legislative and political considerations. Consequently, the present value of cash revenues from a tax rate increase, *PVTR*, will fall within a range bounded by zero at the lower end and an upper limit defined by equation (8).

$$PVTR = \sum_{t=1}^{k} \left[T(1 + i_T)^{t-1} m_{max} (1 + r)^{-t} \right] \tag{8}$$

where T is the municipal tax assessment (the taxable value of the private, nontax-exempt real property in the municipality), i_T is the annual growth rate of the tax assessment, and m_{max} is the maximum permissible increase in the property tax rate, as determined either legislatively or by policy. Since property tax revenues in the current year are based on the previous year's tax assessment, the exponent of the compound growth factor for T is lagged by one year.

The test of program viability under the property tax option entails finding the incremental tax rate, m, that will equate the sum of the present values of the annual cash flows from the incremental tax receipts and the net operating revenues with the present value of the initial capital investment. Solving equation (9) yields the required tax increase.

$$m = PVI - PVNR / \sum_{t=1}^{k} \left[T(1 + i_T)^{t-1} (1 + r)^{-t} \right] \tag{9}$$

If $0 < m < m_{max}$, the program is financially viable with a tax increase of m. If $m > m_{max}$ the maximum allowable tax increase is insufficient to finance the project, and another option must be explored. If $m < 0$, net operating revenues alone are more than adequate to finance the program, and no tax increase is necessary.

Revenue Bonds

An obvious prerequisite to issuing revenue bonds is that the program's net operating revenues must be positive. The amount and timing of the revenue will determine the size of the bond issue, since the debt service obligations take precedence in the use of these funds. Thus, given equal annual debt service payments, A, beginning at the end of $t = 1$, bond issue size, D, is equal to the present value of the stream of payments from $t = 1$ to $t = s$, the bond maturity in years $(s \leq k)$. This in turn is equal to the present value of the program's net operating revenues. Algebraically,

$$A = D \left(r^*/[1 - (1 + r^*)^{-s}] \right) \qquad (10)$$

where r^* is the bond interest rate. The present value of A, discounted at r, is

$$PVA = D \left(r^*/[1 - (1 + r^*)^{-s}] \right) \left([1 - (1 + r)^{-s}]/r \right) \qquad (11)$$

Since PVA must also equal the present value of net operating revenues,

$$PVNR = D \left(r^*/[1 - (1 + r^*)^{-s}] \right) \left([1 - (1 + r)^{-s}]/r \right) \qquad (12)$$

When equation (12) is rearranged to solve for D, the bond issue size is determined directly from equation (13).

$$D = PVNR \left([1 - (1 + r^*)^{-s}]/r^* \right) \left(r/[1 - (1 + r)^{-s}] \right) \qquad (13)$$

If $D < PVI$, operating revenues are inadequate to fully repay principal and interest on the debt issue, and the program fails the test of viability under the revenue bond option.

However, if $D > PVI$, the program will generate revenues in excess of debt service; hence, the project's revenues may be either reduced, by lowering the selling price of the product or service generated by the program, or redirected in part to some other project or cost center. The amount by which annual revenues are in excess of minimum program requirements (AR), and thus can be lowered or transferred, is calculated by substituting the appropriate data into equation (14).

$$AR = [(PVNR - PVI) + (D - PVI)] / \sum_{i}^{k} (1 + r)^{-t} \qquad (14)$$

The value of AR is subtracted from the inflation-adjusted nominal cash flows to arrive at the project's adjusted net cash flows for planning purposes.

General Obligation Bonds

Principal and interest payments on general obligation bonds are paid out of general tax revenues received by the issuing municipality. In most instances, the programs being debt financed are not expected to operate on a better than break-even basis; consequently, this test of program financial viability is similar to that examined under the tax increase option.

Given that the project operates at an annual deficit (i.e., $NR_t < 0$), the size of the bond issue, D, is equal to PVI minus $PVNR$, or the total of the present value of the program's total cash outflows. Substituting $PVI - PVNR$ for $PVNR$ in equation (12) to obtain the present value of the equal annual debt service charges, we get

$$PVI - PVNR = D \left(r^*/[1 - (1 + r^*)^{-s}] \right) \left(1 - (1 + r)^{-s}/r \right) \qquad (15)$$

Substituting the right side of equation (15) into equation (9), and calculating the values over the life of the bond issue, s, rather than the life of the project, k, we can calculate the tax increase needed to support the bond issue from equation (16).

$$m = D \left[\frac{\left(r^*/[1-(1+r^*)^{-s}]\right)\left([1-(1+r)^{-s}]/r\right)}{\sum_{t=1}^{s} [T(1+i_T)^{t-1}(1+r)^{-t}]} \right] \qquad (16)$$

If $m > m_{max}$ the project fails the test of viability.

Combinations of Financing Options and Programs

A municipality often will have occasion to examine several combinations of financing options. For example, programs may be funded with a combination of (1) noncapital sources and either a tax increase or a general obligation bond issue; (2) a tax increase and revenue bond issue; or (3) noncapital sources and a revenue bond issue. The form of the calculations necessary to define the dimensions of the financing package and test for financial viability depends on which options are being combined, as well as which option is designated as the primary funds source and which will finance the residual. For example, if a revenue bond issue is chosen as the primary funds source, to be supplemented with a grant and donated funds to the extent necessary, the procedure is to solve for D in equation (13), substitute D for $PVNR$ in equation (6), and then solve for PVQ and then Q in equation (7). If the noncapital source of funds is in the form of *revenue sharing*, the procedure would be reversed—i.e., the starting point would be equation (6), with D equal to PVQ minus PVI.

Variations on the basic options are likewise possible. For example, a municipality may find it expedient to levy a temporary tax increase for, say, three years, to finance a long-lived program. To shorten the tax revenue stream, equation (9) is merely altered to sum the tax increase over three years (instead of *k* years). The solution will produce a higher millage rate, *m*, than would otherwise be the case, but the pain experienced by the taxpayers would be short-lived.

A municipality may also wish to fund a number of projects, each with its own cash-flow characteristics, out of a single financing plan. The logical approach is, first, to aggregate the program cash flows and test for financial viability. If this first trial fails the test, programs should be removed one by one, beginning with the least desirable, until a feasible financing plan is found. Alternatively, one or more of the programs can be scaled down until the aggregated program package fits the financing plan.

While each of the complications mentioned here would require certain modifications to equations (6) through (16), an exhaustive list of such modifications is not required. In the final analysis, the fiscal officer need only make certain that he or she has correctly specified the modifications to the model in terms of timing and priority before attempting the calculations. In any event, the general rule for setting the priority in the use of funds is that "free" money (in the form of noncapital funds) is always the preferred financing form—provided it is really costless. Free money with strings attached may be more expensive than borrowed money, at least in a qualitative sense.

Financing Temporary Deficits

When an otherwise viable program requires large initial cash outlays and the financing package fails to fully cover these outflows in any given budget period, the resultant cash deficit must obviously be financed. If cash transactions for the program are handled through the municipality's contingency reserve fund or its surplus cash fund, a cash deficit in any year, t, will be covered by liquidating a portion of the reserve's earning assets. The cost of this transaction is the loss of income by the fund over the period during which the program experiences a negative cash flow. Quantitatively, the cost is equal to the cash reserve's rate of return, r, times L_t, the program's cash deficit in year t. Since the earning and borrowing rates (r) are identical, the model outlined earlier automatically compensates for the reserve's loss of income as a result of program deficits; hence, no explicit adjustment is necessary.

If, however, the municipality has no reserve fund and must borrow to cover cash deficits at a rate higher than it is able to earn on cash surpluses, an adjustment to PVI is required in testing for financial viability. Equation (17), from which PVI* (the adjusted present value of the program's initial capital investment) is calculated, replaces equation (1) of the model.

$$PVI^* = PVB + PVE + \sum_{t=1}^{k} [L_t(r' - r)(1 + r)^{-t}] \qquad (17)$$

where r' is the appropriate short- or intermediate-term borrowing rate. The nominal values for L_t are obtained by comparing the nominal values of cash inflows with the inflation-adjusted outflows in each year over the life of the program.

Summary

The purpose of presenting the details of the capital budget planning model in such a rigorous mathematical fashion is to enable the interested reader to fully understand the relationships on which the model is based. In some cases, a municipal government may be forced to operate under unique circumstances that would cause some difficulty in applying the model directly. In these cases, the analyst or decision maker who is familiar with the model's construction can easily introduce necessary modifications that will enable him or her to perform the viability tests on even the most uniquely configured program.

The following chapter applies the model to a hypothetical capital expenditure project. Some of the notations and several of the equations presented here will be used as the bases for the calculations in that illustration; however, in the budget manual presented in Chapter 5, most of these are dropped in favor of nonmathematical notation.

CHAPTER

3

AN ILLUSTRATIVE APPLICATION OF THE MODEL

The abstract model presented in Chapter 2 is brought to life in the context of a city's plan to construct and subsequently operate a municipal zoological park. The case history used here is admittedly contrived in order to improve its potential as a teaching device. Hence, no claim is made for the accuracy of the dollar amounts involved or even their relative proportions. The primary purpose for presenting this illustrative calculation is to demonstrate as clearly and forcefully as possible the basic functions of the model and to illustrate its capacity in dealing with several financing options, both individually and in combination. Thus, total realism in the example is justifiably sacrificed to present the model more completely in its several configurations.

None of the members of the Clayton city council knew how much it would cost and no one was certain whether financing the expenditure would be possible, but the vote to go ahead with the feasibility study for the proposed municipal park was unanimous. In the past, Clayton had never been able to afford much in the way of recreation facilities, but prospects for the community looked bright, and the city council knew the voters would support the project with their tax dollars if necessary.

The site on which the park would be built was formerly the property of a large U.S. corporation that had acquired the land with the intention of building a manufacturing plant. The plant was never constructed, however, and ten years later the corporation decided to donate the land to the city with no strings attached.

To get the project off the ground, the city council decided to investigate building a multipurpose facility whose major feature would be a zoo of rather modest proportions. The site was large enough to also accommodate little league baseball and adult softball diamonds, a soccer field, and extensive picnic areas.

As part of the planning process, the city council wanted to avoid charging admission to the zoo and usage fees for the other facilities. It hoped to raise at least some of the money for park construction through a citywide fund-raising campaign but felt that most of the funding would come from tax revenues or a bond issue. The council therefore instructed the planning committee to evaluate four financing options: (1) voluntary donations; (2) a tax increase and donations; (3) general obligation bonds and donations; and (4) revenue bonds, admission fees, and donations.

Exhibit 3-1 presents the data assembled by the planning committee to support the analysis of the proposed park. The exhibit also contains the data source for each of the planning estimates and the values that will be used to test the project for financial viability under the first financing option— voluntary donations. The data base will be modified as required to test the alternative financing options.

Exhibit 3-1: Planning Estimates for the Clayton City Park

Input Data	Symbol	Timing	Value
From the park consultant:			
1. Contract price for construction	B	year 1 year 2 year 3	$150,000 250,000 400,000
2. Cost of animals and equipment	E	year 3	100,000
3. Operating costs	OC	years 4–9	60,000
4. Planning period	k		9 years
From the city council:			
5. Rate of return available from investment of surplus cash	r	years 1–9	9%
6. Short-term borrowing rate	r'	years 1–9	10%
7. Tax assessment	T	year 0	$33 million
8. Annual growth rate of the tax assessment	i_T	years 1–9	2%
9. Maximum amount of local contributions likely	Q_{max}	years 1–4	$200,000
10. Distribution of donations	b_1	year 1	10%
	b_2	years 1–2	20%
	b_3	years 1–3	30%
	b_4	years 1–4	40%
11. Maximum allowable millage rate increase to support the park	m_{max}	years 1–9	2 mills
From other sources:			
12. Construction cost inflation rate	i_B	years 1–9	18%
13. Animal cost inflation rate	i_E	years 1–9	8%
14. Operating cost inflation rate	i_{OC}	years 1–9	7%
15. Long-term borrowing rate	r^*	years 1–9	7%
16. Bond maturity	s		10 years

Voluntary Donations

While it is obvious from the data presented in Exhibit 3-1 that the $900,000 park cannot be financed with only $200,000 of local donations, it is nevertheless useful to apply the model to the fund-raising option in order to determine the amount of money the city would have to raise in voluntary contributions to construct the park and operate it for a six-year period. This information is likely to be needed if the city were to approach nonlocal donors, such as charitable foundations and federal and state agencies that might offer grants to aid in constructing the park.

The first steps required to determine the total dollar amount needed by the city are presented in Exhibit 3-2, where both the present value of the net investment (PVI) and the present value of net revenues ($PVNR$) are calculated from the data provided in Exhibit 3-1. An inflation rate of zero is used for facilities construction in Part A, since the construction costs are based on a firm price for construction beginning immediately and spanning a three-year period. The costs of purchasing park equipment and the animals for the zoo (Part B) are inflated at the rate of 8%, however, since the actual purchases will be delayed until construction of the animal compounds is completed in year 3.

Since the city council hopes to avoid charging fees for the use of the park, no revenues appear in the calculations in Part D of the table. The net revenues are simply the facility's expected operating costs, shown as negative figures, and the present value of the net revenues ($PVNR$) is therefore also a negative figure.

The compound interest, or inflation, factors (CIF) and present value factors (PVF) used in Exhibit 3-2 and the following exhibits can be found at the end of Chapter 5.

The next step in determining the nominal dollar fund-raising goal (Q) that will completely finance the park's construction and subsequent operation is that of calculating the present value factor, f, using equation (7) developed in the preceding chapter:

$$Q = PVQ/f \qquad (7)$$

This step is illustrated in Exhibit 3-3. Note that the columns (2) through (5) correspond to the percentage distribution of donations (item 10 in Exhibit 3-1).

The sum of the figures in column (8) shows that $f = .84476$. Since the present value of Q, PVQ, equals PVI minus $PVNR$ (see equation (6) in Chapter 2), we can substitute the appropriate values from Exhibits 3-2 and 3-3 into equation (7) and solve for the nominal fund-raising goal, Q:

$$\begin{aligned} Q &= PVQ/f \\ &= (PVI - PVNR)/f \\ &= [\$754{,}179 - (-\$319{,}336)]/.84476 \\ &= \$1{,}073{,}515/.84476 \\ Q &= \$1{,}270{,}793 \end{aligned}$$

In other words, the city council would have to raise a little more than $1.27 million in voluntary donations to completely finance the park, under the assumption that the funds would be received in the proportions given in Exhibit 3-1 and column (6) of Exhibit 3-3. Since the community fund-raising campaign is likely to produce only $200,000, another $1.07 million in gifts, grants, or contributions must be obtained elsewhere. Otherwise, another funding option must be selected.

Property Tax Increase

The incremental millage rate, m, required to fully fund the proposed park can be calculated by solving equation (9) of Chapter 2:

$$m = PVI^* - PVNR/ \sum_{t=1}^{k} \left[T(1 + i_T)^{t-1} (1 + r)^{-t} \right]$$

Exhibit 3-2: Calculation of *PVI* and *PVNR* for Financing Option 1

Part A. Construction Costs:

Year	Cash Outlays	CIF @ 0%	PVF @ 9%	Present Value of Construction Costs
1	$150,000	1.000	.91743	$137,615
2	250,000	1.000	.84168	210,420
3	400,000	1.000	.77218	308,872
				$656,907

Part B. Cost of Animals and Park Equipment:

Year	Cash Outlays	CIF @ 8%	PVF @ 9%	Present Value of Cost of Animals
3	$100,000	1.2597	.77218	$97,272

Part C. *PVI* = Present value of construction costs plus present value of the cost of animals and equipment.

= $656,907 + $97,272
= $754,179

ILLUSTRATIVE APPLICATION OF THE MODEL/37

Part D. Net Revenues:

Year	Operating Costs	CIF @ 7%	PVF @ 9%	Present Value of Net Revenues
4	$60,000	1.3108	.70843	$ (55,717)
5	60,000	1.4026	.64993	(54,696)
6	60,000	1.5007	.59627	(53,689)
7	60,000	1.6058	.54703	(52,705)
8	60,000	1.7182	.50187	(51,739)
9	60,000	1.8385	.46043	(50,790)
				PVNR = $(319,336)

Exhibit 3-3: Calculation of the Present Value Factor, f

(1) Year	(2) b_1	(3) $1/2 b_2$	(4) $1/3 b_3$	(5) $1/4 b_4$	(6) (2)+(3)+(4)+(5)	(7) PVF @ 9%	(8) (6)×(7)
1	.10				.40	.91743	.36697
2		.10	.10	.10	.30	.84168	.25250
3		.10	.10	.10	.20	.77218	.15444
4			.10	.10	.10	.70843	.07084
	.10	.20	.30	.40	1.00		$f =$ .84476

where PVI^* is defined as the present value of the net investment *minus* the present value of the maximum amount of donated funds. In this case,

$$
\begin{aligned}
PVI^* &= PVI - PVQ_{max} \\
&= PVI - fQ_{max} \\
&= \$754{,}179 - (.84476 \times \$200{,}000) \\
PVI^* &= \$585{,}227
\end{aligned}
$$

Here we have assumed that the community fund-raising campaign will produce $200,000 and that the timing of these cash inflows will agree with the schedule contained in Exhibit 3-3. The balance of the proposed project, totaling $585,227, will be funded with the proceeds of the property tax increase.

The denominator of equation (9) is calculated as shown in Exhibit 3-4 from the data provided in Exhibit 3-1. The total of column (5) is the present value of the tax assessment adjusted for its assumed 2% annual growth rate.

The incremental millage rate needed to fully fund the project as it is currently planned is found by substituting the values previously calculated for PVI^* and $PVNR$ into the numerator of equation (9), substituting the sum of column (5) of Exhibit 3-4 into the denominator of that equation, and solving for m:

$$
\begin{aligned}
m &= (\$585{,}227 + \$319{,}336)/\$212{,}024{,}357 \\
&= \$904{,}563/\$212{,}024{,}357 \\
m &= .004266 \text{ or } 4.266 \text{ mills}
\end{aligned}
$$

Since the Clayton city council has limited the millage rate increase in support of this project to 2 mills, the property tax increase is not a viable alternative, even considering the $200,000 of donated funds. Exhibit 3-5 presents the project's cash flows, given that the city council decided to increase property taxes by 4.266 mills—the "answer" given by the model. The figures in the table demonstrate that the combination of donated funds and the tax increase will fully

ILLUSTRATIVE APPLICATION OF THE MODEL/39

Exhibit 3-4: **Present Value of Clayton's Tax Assessment**

(1) Year	(2) Tax Assessment	(3) CIF @ 2%*	(4) PVF @ 9%	(5) (2) × (3) × (4)
1	$33,000,000	1.0000	.91743	$ 30,275,190
2	33,000,000	1.0200	.84168	28,330,948
3	33,000,000	1.0404	.77218	26,511,410
4	33,000,000	1.0612	.70843	24,808,935
5	33,000,000	1.0824	.64993	23,214,979
6	33,000,000	1.1041	.59627	21,725,276
7	33,000,000	1.1262	.54703	20,330,151
8	33,000,000	1.1487	.50187	19,024,436
9	33,000,000	1.1717	.46043	17,803,032
				$212,024,357

* The CIFs are lagged one year, since the tax assessment of the prior year is used to compute the current year's tax receipts.

Sources of data:

Column	Source
(2)	Exhibit 3-1, item 7.
(3)	Exhibit A, end of Chapter 5.
(4)	Exhibit C, end of Chapter 5.

fund the park, since the ending cash balance drops to zero (or very close to zero) in the last year of the planning period. However, since the ending cash balances for years 3 through 8, listed in column (8) of the table, are negative, the city will have to raise some additional money to pay the interest on the funds it will have to borrow to keep the project operating. The cash balance deficits at the end of each year can be financed either internally, by borrowing from available cash surpluses, or externally, by borrowing from a bank on a short-term basis. Short-term borrowing can be used since property tax receipts generally are received at one time during the year and are spent gradually over the entire fiscal year. The surplus can be used to repay borrowed sums and the loan renewed when the surplus is depleted.

Since the short-term borrowing rate is 10%, the city will

Exhibit 3-5: Cash Flow Analysis of the Tax Increase Option at 4.266 Mills

(1) Year	(2) Tax Receipts @ 4.266 Mills	(3) Building and Operating Costs	(4) Donated Funds	(5) Nominal Net Cash Flow (2) + (3) + (4)	(6) Initial Cash Balance	(7) Interest Earned (6) × .09	(8) Ending Cash Balance (5) + (6) + (7)
1	$140,778	$ -150,000	$80,000	$ 70,778	0	0	$ 70,778
2	143,594	-250,000	60,000	-46,406	$ 70,778	$ 6,370	30,742
3	146,465	-525,970	40,000	-339,505	30,742	2,767	-305,996
4	149,394	-78,648	20,000	90,746	-305,996	-27,540	-242,790
5	152,378	-84,156		68,222	-242,790	-21,851	-196,419
6	155,433	-90,042		65,391	-196,419	-17,678	-148,706
7	158,544	-96,348		62,196	-148,706	-13,384	-99,894
8	161,712	-103,092		58,620	-99,894	-8,990	-50,264
9	164,950	-110,310		54,640	-50,264	-4,524	-148*

* Does not equal zero because of rounding errors.

Sources of data:

Column	Source
(2)	Column (2) × column (3) in Exhibit 3-4, times 4.266 mills.
(3)	Exhibit 3-2, all figures are inflation-adjusted.
(4)	Exhibit 3-1, items 9 and 10.
(6)	Assumes no cash is on hand to begin the project.

have to pay a premium of one percentage point over the rate earned on its surplus cash account (10% − 9%) for the money it borrows in support of the project. Exhibit 3-6 illustrates the method used to calculate the present value of the incremental interest cost.

The figures in column (2) in Exhibit 3-6 are taken from column (8) in Exhibit 3-5. These are the year-end negative balances in the project's cash surplus "account." The incremental interest cost of 1% times the amounts borrowed in each year is discounted at the rate r (9%). The total of the present values in column (5) represents the amount needed at present ($t = 0$) to cover the incremental interest cost incurred as a result of the project's cash-flow pattern.

The present value of the incremental interest cost, $7,044, may be added to PVI^* in equation (9) in order to recalculate the millage rate, m, needed to finance the project in its entirety. In this case,

m = ($585,227 + $319,336 + $7,044)/$212,024,357
m = 4.3 mills

The extra interest cost added about .034 mills to the rate originally calculated.

General Obligation Bonds

Since the Clayton city council is hoping to avoid charging admission and park-usage fees, general obligation bonds (or a term loan from a bank, insurance company, or other lender) may prove to be a feasible method of financing the project. The city will continue to rely on the community fund-raising campaign to partially finance the park, and it pledges a maximum of 2 mills of the tax assessment in support of debt service on a ten-year, 7% bond issue or loan.

The analysis of this funding alternative begins by calcu-

Exhibit 3-6: **Present Value of Incremental Interest Costs**

(1) Year	(2) Amount Borrowed	(3) Incremental Interest Cost (2) × .01	(4) PVF @ 9%	(5) Present Value of Incremental Interest (3) × (4)
3	$305,996	$3,060	.77218	$2,363
4	242,790	2,428	.70843	1,720
5	196,419	1,964	.64993	1,276
6	148,706	1,487	.59627	887
7	99,894	999	.54703	546
8	50,264	503	.50187	252
				$7,044

Sources of data:

Column	Source
(2)	Exhibit 3-5, Column (8).
(3)	Interest cost = borrowing rate minus investing rate.
(4)	Exhibit C, end of Chapter 5.

lating PVI^* in the same way it was done in the property tax increase option; that is,

$$
\begin{aligned}
PVI^* &= PVI - PVQ_{max} \\
&= PVI - fQ_{max} \\
&= \$754{,}170 - (.84476 \times \$200{,}000) \\
PVI^* &= \$585{,}227
\end{aligned}
$$

The size of the bond issue or principal amount of the loan, D, is equal to the present value of the project's total net cash outflows, which in turn is equal to PVI^* minus $PVNR$; thus,

$$
\begin{aligned}
D &= PVI^* - PVNR \\
&= \$585{,}227 - (-\$319{,}336) \\
D &= \$904{,}563
\end{aligned}
$$

ILLUSTRATIVE APPLICATION OF THE MODEL/43

The millage rate needed to support a bond issue of this size is calculated using equation (16) in Chapter 2:

$$m = D \left[\frac{\left(r^*/[1-(1+r^*)^{-s}]\right)\left([1-(1+r)^{-s}]/r\right)}{\sum_{t=1}^{s} [T(1+i_T)^{t-1}(1+r)^{-t}]} \right] \quad (16)$$

Exhibit 3-1 lists the long-term borrowing rate, r^*, as 7% and the bond maturity, s, as ten years. Thus, the first fraction in the numerator of equation (16),

$$r^*/[1-(1+r^*)^{-s}]$$

which is a present value factor that represents the annual payment needed to retire $1 of bond principal plus interest at r^* percent over s years, is equal to 0.14238 for a 7% bond issue or loan having a ten-year maturity. The value of the fraction is calculated as follows:

$$\begin{aligned}
PVF &= r^*/[1-(1/[1+r^*]^s)] \\
&= .07/[1-(1/[1+.07]^{10})] \\
&= .07/(1/1.96715) \\
&= .07/(1-.50835) = .07/.49165 \\
PVF &= 0.14238
\end{aligned}$$

The other fraction in the numerator of equation (16), calculated in a similar manner, is equal to 6.4177. The value for the denominator of equation (16),

$$\left(\sum_{t=1}^{s} [T(1+i_T)^{t-1}(1+r)^{-t}] \right)$$

has been calculated in Exhibit 3-4, thereby producing the following values that are substituted in calculating m:

$$m = (\$904{,}563 \times 0.14238 \times 6.4177)/\$212{,}024{,}357$$
$$m = .0039 \text{ or } 3.9 \text{ mills}$$

which is again greater than the maximum millage rate of 2 mills set by the city council. The park still appears to be a nonviable project. However, we can gain a little more information by rearranging equation (16) in the following way:

$$m_{max} = .002 = (D_{max} \times 0.14238 \times 6.4177)/\$212{,}024{,}357$$

By solving for D_{max}, the maximum amount the city can borrow based on a 2-mill tax increase, the city council can calculate the shortage of funds faced by the park project. Thus,

$$D_{max} = (.002 \times \$212{,}024{,}357)/(0.14238 \times 6.4177)$$
$$D_{max} = \$464{,}074$$

which is ($904,563 − $464,074 =) $440,489 short of the total dollar amount needed immediately to fully fund the new city park.

Revenue Bonds

The preceding tests for financial viability should clearly indicate that the city council's preliminary decision to avoid imposing admission charges and park-usage fees will have to be set set aside if the park, as it is presently conceived, is going to be made financially viable. Let us assume, therefore, that the council changes its mind and establishes a fees structure that will generate annual revenues of $90,000 beginning in year 4. We will also assume that the revenues

ILLUSTRATIVE APPLICATION OF THE MODEL/45

will increase at a compound rate of 4% per year thereafter as the number of visitors increases. Donations will be solicited as before. Exhibit 3-7 recalculates *PVNR*, using the data provided in Exhibit 3-2, part *D*, for the present value of operating costs.

By substituting the total of the figures in column (7) of Exhibit 3-7 into equation (13) (Chapter 2), the city council can calculate the size of the revenue bond issue that the project can support out of the revenues it promises to generate. The revenue bonds will carry a 7% interest rate and mature serially over ten years.

$$D = PVNR \left([1 - (1 + r^*)^{-s}]/r^*\right) \left(r/[1 - (1 + r)^{-s}]\right) \quad (13)$$
$$= \$21,941 \times 7.02346 \times 0.15582$$
$$D = \$24,012$$

Since *PVI**, calculated earlier, is $585,227, revenue bonds obviously cannot provide adequate funds for the project. The park project's anticipated revenues are simply too small to repay the initial investment in construction, equipment, and animals.

To make the revenue bond option viable, the project's annual (nominal) revenues after inflation must be increased by an amount, *AR*, calculated using equation (14) (Chapter 2).

$$AR = \left[(PVNR - PVI) + (D - PVI)\right] / \sum_{j}^{k} (1 + r)^{-t} \quad (14)$$
$$= \left[(\$21,941 - \$585,227) + \$24,012 - \$585,227)\right]/3.46396$$
$$= \$ -1,124,501/3.46396$$
$$AR = \$ -324,629$$

Note: The negative sign in the answer may be ignored, since *AR* is defined as the amount by which revenues can be *lowered* to achieve an exact equality between *D* and *PVI**. Used in this way, *AR* must be *lowered* by a *negative* amount—in other words, *increased*.

Exhibit 3-7: **Recalculation of PVNR for the Revenue Bond Option**

(1) Year	(2) Present Value of Operating Costs	(3) Revenues	(4) CIF @ 4%*	(5) PVF @ 9%	(6) Present Value of Revenues (3) × (4) × (5)	(7) PVNR (6) − (2)
4	$55,717	$90,000	1.0000	.70843	$63,759	$ 8,042
5	54,696	90,000	1.0400	.64993	60,833	6,137
6	53,689	90,000	1.0816	.59627	58,043	4,354
7	52,705	90,000	1.1249	.54703	55,382	2,677
8	51,739	90,000	1.1699	.50187	52,842	1,103
9	50,790	90,000	1.2167	.46043	50,418	−372
						$21,941

* Compound growth of revenues begins in year 5.

Sources of data:

Column	Source
(2)	Exhibit 3-2, part D.
(3)	Given.
(4)	Exhibit A, end of Chapter 5.
(5)	Exhibit C, end of Chapter 5.

In this case, revenues in year 4 (the first year of the park's operations) must be ($324,629 + $90,000 =) $414,629, or about four and one-half times greater than planned by the city council.

Summary of the Data

Although the results of the application of the model to the Clayton City Park project may be personally disappointing to the city council, no doubt should remain that the project, as it is presently conceived, is simply too costly for the city's current financial circumstances. However, the data generated by the model provide certain insights into the project's cash-flow characteristics and, hence, into ways in which it can be modified to make it financially viable.

Exhibit 3-8 summarizes the relevant data provided by the city park application of the model. It reveals that the general obligation bond option can fund about half of the project and comes the closest of all the alternatives to providing financial viability. If the city council will relax its prohibition on charging admission and usage fees, it may retest the third alternative. Since $PVNR$ with $90,000 of revenues equals $21,941,

$$
\begin{aligned}
D &= PVI^* - PVNR \\
&= \$585,227 - \$21,941 \\
D &= \$563,286
\end{aligned}
$$

The millage rate required to support the bond issue therefore can be lowered to

$$
\begin{aligned}
m &= (\$563,286 \times 0.14238 \times 6.4177)/\$212,024,357 \\
m &= 2.428 \text{ mills}
\end{aligned}
$$

While the addition of the admission and usage fees to the project's revenue stream will still not make general obligation

Exhibit 3-8: **Summary of Clayton's Four Financing Options**

Financing Alternative	Constraint on Viability	Amount Needed to Achieve Viability
Voluntary donations	$200,000	$1,270,793
Tax increase	2-mill increase	4.3 mills
General obligation bonds	2-mill increase	3.9 mills
Revenue bonds	$90,000 per year in revenues	$414,629 per year in revenues

bonds a viable option, the target tax increase is now only 0.428 mills over the maximum limit of 2 mills. The project's revenues likewise place the project closer to being made financially viable if additional voluntary contributions can be obtained.

Finally, the data reveal that viability can be achieved if the initial investment, or cost of the project, can be reduced. Thus, rather than providing a go/no-go decision, the planning model provides a method of testing for viability, indicates where modifications to the plan can make the greatest impact, and allows for retesting until the project's dimensions meet the critical standards for financial viability. This aspect of the model will be more fully explored in the next chapter.

CHAPTER 4

OTHER FEATURES OF THE MODEL

The example presented in Chapter 2 demonstrated the Capital Budget Planning Model's versatility in dealing with alternative financing options. This chapter presents the model's versatility in several other dimensions, such as its ability to analyze the effects of delaying project implementation on financial viability and its capacity to handle variables whose future values are uncertain or subject to some degree of volatility. The chapter concludes with a discussion of how the model's output can be used to control both project expenditures and the continuing operation of the project over its expected life.

Once the user has become acquainted with the way in which the the model works by applying it to several projects with which he or she is familiar, the model's versatility will become evident. As project data are run through the model and results are obtained, additional questions beginning with the words "What if . . ." will occur to those involved in project planning. In most cases the model will be able to provide the answers to these questions in terms of the effects any changes in the project will have on its financial viability. The following discussion will serve as a primer in this regard.

Project Timing

The Clayton city council planned the park project described in Chapter 3 under the assumption that construction would start immediately. While that assumption probably is appropriate for most municipal capital expenditure proposals, situations often occur in which the governing body may wish to examine the effects of delaying program implementation for one or more years. The wisdom of considering such a delay is dependent on certain of the model's key variables, the most important of which are the inflation rates of construction, equipment, and operating costs. Other factors that may also significantly affect the financial implications of delaying the project are the relevant interest rates, the distribution of cash donations between immediate gifts and future pledges, and the dollar amount of the project's initial investment.

Exhibits 4-1, 4-2, and 4-3 portray graphically the changes in the property tax rate that would result from delaying construction of the park up to the tenth year. The calculations on which these figures are based assume that a tax increase alone will fund the project. Certain variations from the data base presented in Exhibit 3-1 are assumed in the calculations on which Exhibits 4-2 and 4-3 are based. These are explained in the text that follows.

Rising Project Costs

Exhibit 4-1 presents what is currently the most likely outcome of delaying the park project from one to ten years, given the following planning estimates from the example in Chapter 3:

1. Construction inflation rate	18%
2. Animal and equipment inflation rate	8%
3. Operating cost inflation rate	7%
4. Tax assessment growth	2%
5. Rate of return on surplus cash	9%

OTHER FEATURES OF THE MODEL/51

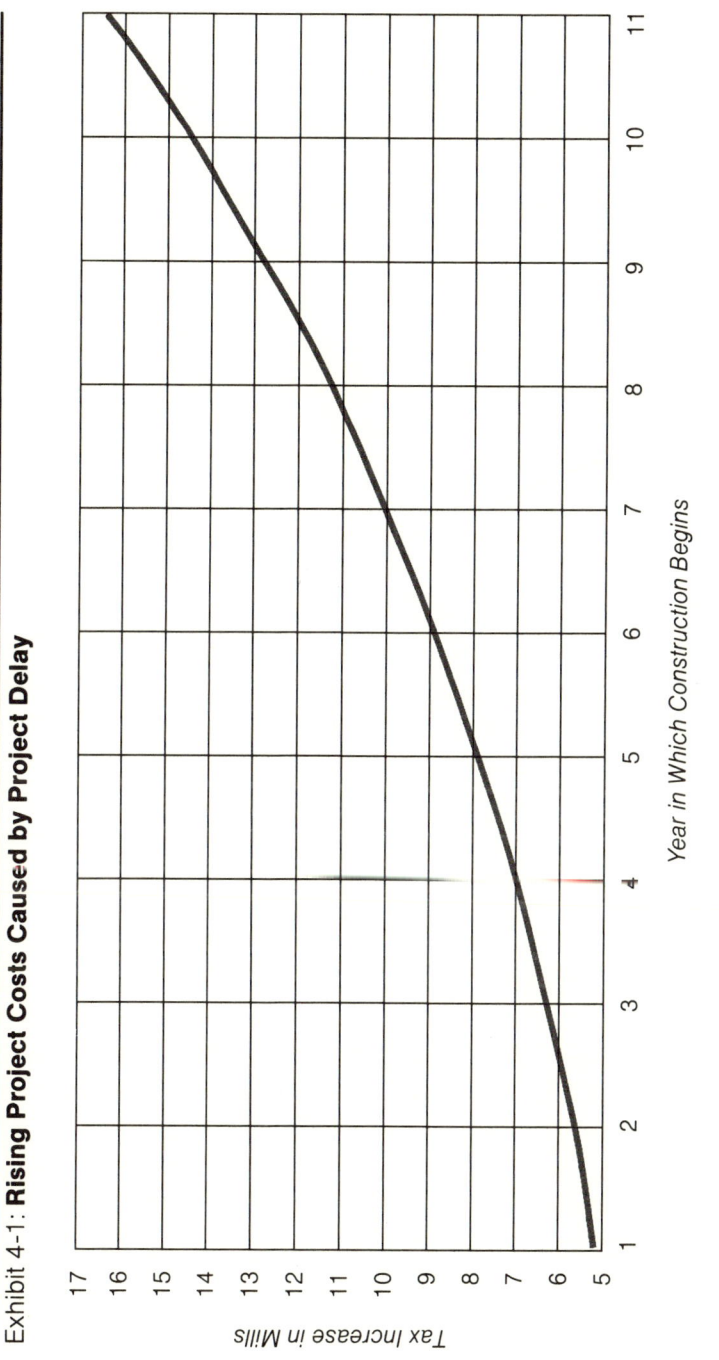

Exhibit 4-1: **Rising Project Costs Caused by Project Delay**

The high rates of inflation for construction, equipment, and operating costs tend to make the project more expensive to build and operate in the future. The incremental tax increase required to fund the city park rises dramatically as implementing the project is postponed year after year. Thus, the best time to begin construction is immediately, insofar as cost minimization is concerned.

Falling Project Costs

The situation illustrated in Exhibit 4-2 is the reverse of that depicted in Exhibit 4-1; the construction and animal and equipment inflation rates were reduced to zero and the operating cost inflation rate was cut to 1.5%, with all other planning estimates remaining constant. The effect of these changes is a continuing reduction in the millage rate as postponement of the project continues.

But an indefinite postponement of project implementation is obviously an unreasonable solution for a municipality with urgent facilities requirements, no matter how tight its budgetary situation may be. The real benefit from calculating the results of successive delays, therefore, is that they reveal the magnitude of the changes in the required millage rate as a result of project postponement. The fiscal officer can use these data to help decide the appropriate trade-off between delaying the start of the project (and the benefits the project will produce) and decreasing the property tax millage rate. As Exhibit 4-2 reveals, delaying the project for two years (until year 3) will reduce the property tax rate increase by 0.145 mills, from 4.539 to 4.394 mills. This represents a reduction of $5.80 in the tax increase that would be levied on an $80,000 house that is taxed at 50% of its value, thus reducing the total tax increase from $181.56 to $175.76 on that property. In this case the delay does not seem to produce significant savings for the home owner.

OTHER FEATURES OF THE MODEL / 53

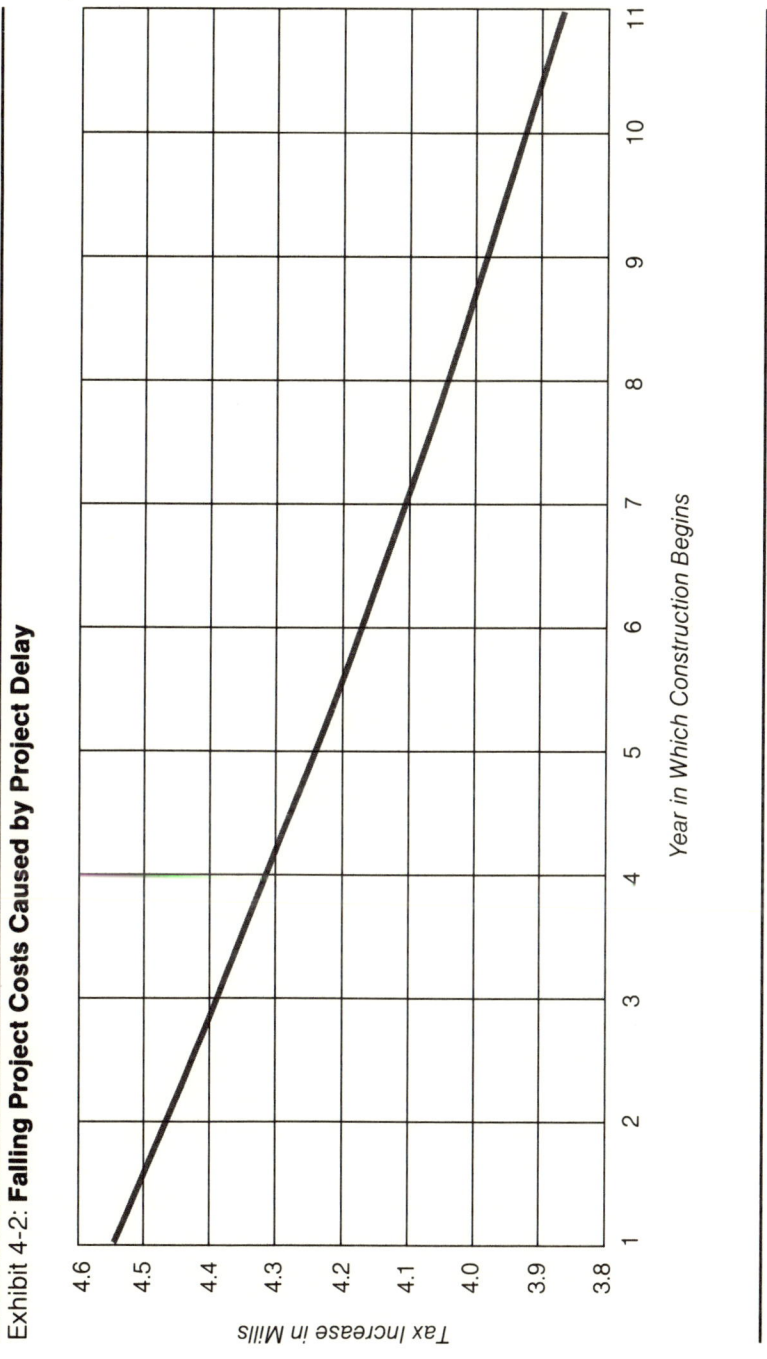

Exhibit 4-2: **Falling Project Costs Caused by Project Delay**

Cost Minimization

In some cases a true minimum tax increase can be achieved by delaying project implementation. Several combinations of data values will produce a U-shaped relationship between the length of a delay and the tax increase required to fully fund the project. Exhibit 4-3 presents such a curve resulting from a low construction inflation rate (1.5%), high rates of inflation for equipment (10%) and operating costs (15.5%), a high growth rate in the tax assessment (9.5%), and a moderate return on surplus cash (8%). This combination of planning estimates suggests that project implementation should be delayed until year 5 in order to minimize the required tax increase. Of course, if the principal societal objective of the project dominates financial considerations, the project can be implemented immediately with a difference of only 0.16 mills between the current millage rate increase and the true minimum.

Uncertainty

Although the future cannot be predicted with absolute certainty, the capital budget planning model assumes that the values for all input data are known in advance. The "answers" it produces, such as those contained in the discussion of the financing options in Chapter 3, are based on that assumption. However, the model provides a way to test the certainty assumption by allowing the user to consider ranges of planning values for the projects. The difficulty with using ranges of data, of course, is that the number of calculations required to fully explore all possible future values for each variable can be overwhelming.

Fortunately, many municipalities have microcomputers that can be used to take the drudgery out of the number crunching required in any sort of financial planning. Chapter 6 presents a computer-aided version of the model; however,

OTHER FEATURES OF THE MODEL/**55**

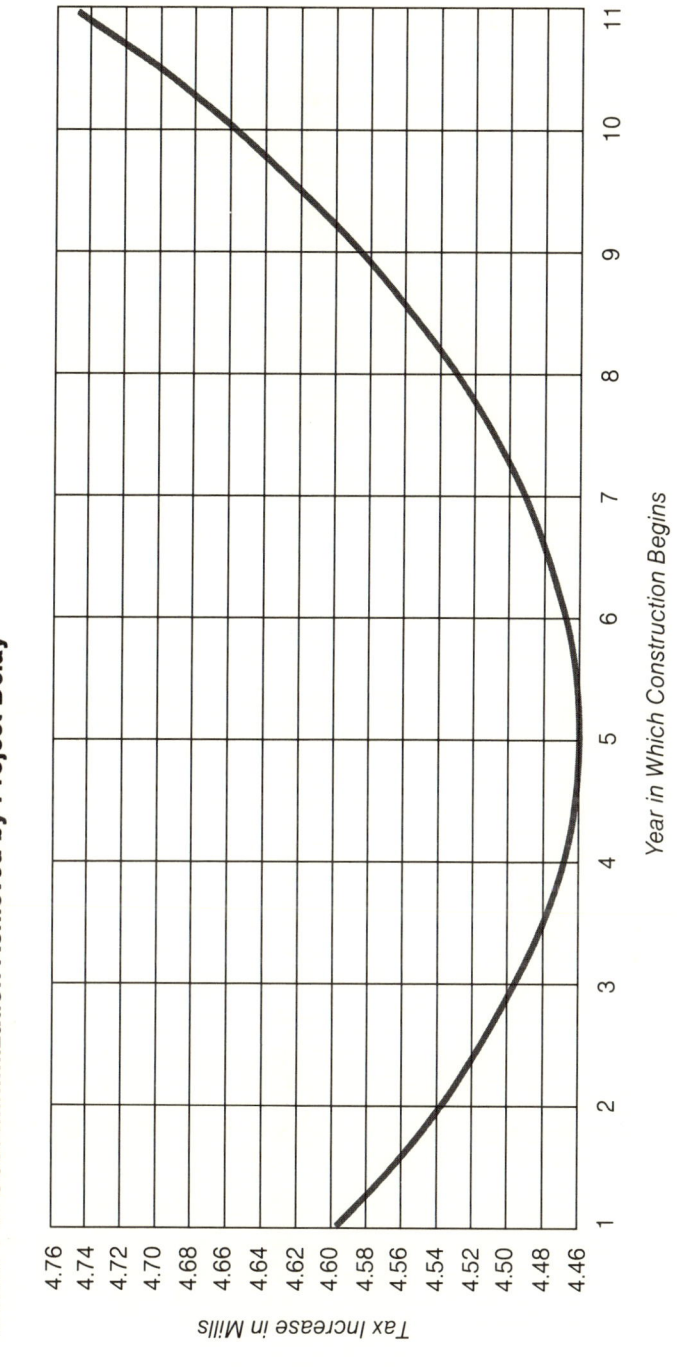

Exhibit 4-3: **Cost Minimization Achieved by Project Delay**

to use these tools efficiently, the user should have a plan before he or she does any planning. Thus, by careful selection of the variables to be examined and the ranges of values that will bracket their expected future values, the planner can significantly reduce the time spent on dealing with uncertainty. An example will help illustrate this technique.

Continuing with the Clayton City Park example presented in the previous chapter, we will assume that the city council has decided to fund the project with an increase in property taxes alone. But during the analysis of the project, the fiscal officer expressed serious reservations as to the accuracy of three planning variables in particular: the inflation rate of equipment and animal purchases (i_E); the operating cost inflation rate (i_{OC}); and the rate of return on the cash reserve fund (r).

To test the sensitivity of the millage rate needed to fully fund the park project to changes in these variables, the property tax option is recomputed, first, by using high and low estimates for each variable in turn, holding the other variables constant and, second, by using high and low estimates of all three planning variables in combination. Exhibit 4-4 presents the results of the sensitivity analysis. In parts A, B, and C of the exhibit, all other variables are held constant at their values given in Exhibit 3-1, while the planning variable being examined is given its high and low values, respectively. Parts D and E show the combined effects of simultaneously setting the three variables at their extreme values.

The level of the millage rate for this particular example is least sensitive to changes in the equipment and animal inflation rate, thus making an accurate forecast of these costs relatively unimportant; an error of 4 percentage points in either direction produces a maximum error of only six-hundredths of 1 mill in the required tax rate. Operating cost inflation, however, requires an accurate forecast, since it produces a more than three-quarters of 1 mill change in

Exhibit 4-5: **Cash-flow Control Report for the City Park Under the Voluntary Donations Option, After One Year of Operation**

(1)	Inflation-adjusted Cash Outflows			Cash Inflows From Fund Raising			
	(2)	(3)	(4)	(5)	(6)	(7)	(8)
Project Year	Budget	Actual	Variance (2) – (3)	Budget	Actual	Variance (6) – (5)	Program Surplus (Deficit) (4) + (7)
1	$150,000	$150,983	$(983)	$508,319	$499,609	$(8,710)	$(9,693)
2	250,000			381,239			
3	525,971			254,239			
4	78,648			127,080			
5	84,153			0			
6	90,044			0			
7	96,347			0			
8	103,091			0			
9	110,307			0			

the tax rate with an increase of from 4% to 12% in the "price level."

Interestingly, in this example, increases in the interest rate, r, produce *increases* in the required millage rate. This is because the park project will operate with negative ending cash balances in each year (see Exhibit 3-5). The park will have to pay the interest on those deficits at the rate r in order to prevent the city from losing the income that the cash surplus otherwise would have provided. Thus, the higher the return available from the cash surplus, the more costly will be the project. Alternatively, if a project generates cash surpluses, the effect of an increase in r will be opposite to that noted here.

Parts D and E of Exhibit 4-4 show that the resultant property tax increase varies by more than 1 mill between the most favorable and least favorable probable future states of nature. Thus, the city council may wish to take a conservative position and add a fraction of a mill onto the tax rate increase offered by the combination of the planning variable values deemed "most likely" to occur during the life of the park project. In this way, the project will generate surplus revenues if all goes well and will not fare too badly in case the actual inflation rates exceed the planners' estimates.

Budgetary Controls

Another feature of the capital budget planning model is its ability to produce data that are useful for controlling both the funding and the implementation phases of the project. A cash-flow forecast, such as the one presented in Exhibit 4-5, can serve as a gross check on the project's cash inflows and outflows. Variations occurring in actual experience will serve as signals that the desired results are not being achieved.

The figures in budget columns (2) and (5) (Exhibit 4-5)

represent the park's expected cash flows under the voluntary donations option, assuming, of course, that the city will be able to raise the entire $1,270,793 from gifts and grants. To benefit from this control device, the city should maintain accounting records on a program basis to accumulate the data recorded in the *actual* columns (3) and (6), as shown in Exhibit 4-5.

Assume that *actual* cash outflows and donations received by the end of the first year of the project's life were $150,903 and $499,609, respectively. Under these circumstances, the project will suffer *unfavorable* variances (adverse cash flows) in both the cash outflow and fund-raising variance columns (4) and (7), resulting in an overall program deficit of $9,693 for the first year. This amount, plus one year's interest

Exhibit 4-4: **Sensitivity Analysis Performed on Three Variables**

	Variable	Estimated Value	Required Millage Rate Increase (in mills)
A.	i_E	4%	5.014
	i_E	8	5.063
	i_E	12	5.120
B.	i_{OC}	4	4.182
	i_{OC}	7	5.063
	i_{OC}	12	5.585
C.	r	6	4.929
	r	9	5.063
	r	12	5.197
D.	i_E	4	
	i_{OC}	4	4.608
	r	6	
E.	i_E	12	
	i_{OC}	12	5.740
	r	12	

(calculated at the rate of return realized from the investment of surplus cash) must be generated in year 2 by either reducing operating costs, increasing donations, or both, in order to keep the project financially viable.

In other words, to keep the city's cash position from deteriorating because the park was built, the project manager must generate a surplus of $9,693 plus ($9,693 × .09 =) $872 by the end of the second project year. Failing this, he or she must modify future plans to reduce operating costs or secure some other source of financing, the exact amounts of which can be determined by replacing forecasted cash flows with actual cash flows and once again working through the capital budgeting planning model.

Aid to Cash Management

Finally, another important benefit can be derived from making explicit cash flow forecasts, such as those provided in Exhibit 3-5. This benefit accrues to the city's cash management effort by providing a basis for investment portfolio maturity decisions. Knowledge of the timing, magnitude, and direction of cash flows permits the fiscal officer to properly schedule maturities of security purchases and provides sufficient advance warning to permit the orderly liquidation of investments (or the maintenance of adequate liquidity) to correspond with cash needs as and when they arise. Such information facilitates portfolio management by permitting the city's available cash surpluses to be more fully invested in longer maturity (higher yielding) investment securities as well as minimizing the proportion of total assets held in very liquid forms as a defense against uncertainties in cash flow.

Summary

The primary purpose of this chapter was to demonstrate the versatility of the capital budget planning model beyond its role as a basis for judging long-run financial viability on a program basis. By implication, this chapter has strongly suggested that the model is not merely a mechanical tool that automatically signals go or no-go after the data are estimated. Instead, it is a tool for *analyzing* all of the financial aspects of a proposed, long-run project and *assisting* the municipal governing body in arriving at a decision that will accomplish its immediate objectives without also imposing future financial penalties on the municipality's operating budget or its taxpayers.

The important ancillary considerations in analyzing capital investment projects are project timing, dealing with uncertain cash flows, using budgetary controls, and assisting the municipality's cash management effort. Each of these considerations extend the usefulness of the model in the area of municipal financial management.

CHAPTER

A CAPITAL BUDGET MODEL FOR SMALL CITY AND COUNTY GOVERNMENTS

This chapter presents and illustrates the use of a Capital Budget Planning Manual designed particularly for small counties and cities (population of 10,000 or less) that do not have ready access to computer equipment or services. The manual is neither an extension nor reformulation of the model presented in the preceding chapters; rather it is merely a translation of the mathematical notation of the model into the more familiar Accounting format. The purpose of this manual, like the model itself, is to assist the municipal fiscal officer in analyzing a wide range of proposed capital investments (or other noncapital, long-lived programs) for the purpose of planning for financial viability of each project examined.

The capital budget planning model can be applied to a municipal project either manually, with the aid of a pocket or desktop calculator, or with the help of a microcomputer. Chapter 6 presents the computer-assisted version of the model, while this chapter contains a capital budget manual that permits the planner to work through the analysis of a capital investment by filling in and performing calculations on a number of accounting-type forms.

The capital budget manual, which begins on page 67, is divided into five parts, each of which is presented and discussed separately in the context of the now familiar Clayton City Park example. While the manual cannot be made specific enough in its design to cover all the possible project configurations that municipalities are likely to encounter in actual application, every effort has been made to clarify the methodology so that the user will encounter a minimum of difficulty in adapting the manual to meet his or her specific (and often unique) planning needs. Thus, the key to successful application of the financial viability concept is to carefully follow the calculations presented in the manual, step by step. By so doing, the reader should be able to gain a thorough understanding of the purpose, data requirements, and methodology of each of the manual's five parts. Those who plan to use the computer-assisted version of the model should likewise work carefully through the manual to gain some insight into the way in which the model works.

The capital budget manual's five parts are:
1. Program description
2. Inflation and interest rate adjustments
3. Financial viability tests:
    a. Gifts and grants
    b. Tax revenues
    c. Revenue bonds
    d. General obligation bonds
4. Cash-flow characteristics
5. Project controls

The organization of the manual closely parallels that presented in Chapter 3. Thus, the comprehension of the methodology in the budget manual format will aid comprehension of the model itself and greatly expand its potential usefulness in actual application "back home."

The manual was designed to be self-contained. Each form on which information is recorded or calculations are performed is preceded by a brief description of that form and followed by a set of detailed instructions for its proper completion. Again, since it is impossible to anticipate all of the variations among projects for which the manual will be used, the reader will have to depend on his or her knowledge of the model itself to provide guidance in those cases in which the manual's instructions may be incomplete or unclear.

The careful reader will note that the "answers" supplied by the manual are not the same as those provided in Chapter 3. This is because the project's life has been extended for *one additional year* in the manual's example, and some of the options are in slightly modified form.

A Capital Budget Manual for Small City and County Governments

©1980, 1987 by Dr. Richard F. Wacht
Finance Department
College of Business Administration
Georgia State University
Atlanta, Georgia

Part 1. Program Description

Definition
The program description is a financial, economic, and operating profile of the planned project.

Format
Questionnaire

Purpose
Its purpose is to guide the financial officer in the gathering and preparation of the relevant project data in the precise form in which the manual will use the data. It also serves as the base document for project review in the "control" phase of the planning process. That is, once the project is in operation, the *Program Description* is used to determine the causes of observed budget variances. More will be said about this later.

Sources of Data
The data requested in the *Program Description* will come from a number of sources with which you are already familiar and from some sources that may be somewhat foreign to you. The *Supplement* to the *Program Description* form describes the sources you will normally consult in gathering the data; however, chances are that you will have to explore many alternative sources before the job is complete.

Remember, this first step is critical. If the figures recorded on this form are grossly inaccurate, the results produced ultimately to aid your decision-making process will be all but worthless. Thus, it is extremely important that your information input be as accurate as possible. However, do not be alarmed if the best you can do is to produce an "informed guess" for any of these data requirements; the performance of *sensitivity analysis* will help nullify the problems arising from this kind of uncertainty.

Program Description

Project Title *J. Wellington Doss Memorial Park*

A. Year in which project implementation is scheduled to begin *1981* (first year)
   Current year (initial planning year) *1980*

B. Capital costs
   1. a. Contract price of construction $666,670
      b. Cost of approved changes   —
      c. Total of lines 1a and 1b $666,670
      d. 20% of line 1c for engineering
         and contingency costs   *133,330*
      e. Capital costs, total of lines 1c
         and 1d $800,000

   2. Schedule of payments for capital costs:
      a. First year   1*981*   *$150,000*
      b. Second year   1*982*   *250,000*
      c. Third year   1*983*   *400,000*
      d. Fourth year   1*984*   —
      e. Total of lines 2a, b, c, d $800,000

C. Equipment costs
   1. Schedule of equipment purchases:
      a. First year   1*981* $ —
      b. Second year   1*982*   —
      c. Third year   1*983*   *100,000*
      d. Fourth year   1*984*   —
      e. Total of lines 1a, b, c, d   *$100,000*

D. Operating costs and revenues
   1. Schedule of annual operating costs and revenues covering the life of the project.

70/CAPITAL BUDGETING FOR CITY AND COUNTY GOVERNMENTS

Year	Operation and Maintenance Costs	Desired Surplus from Operations	Operating and Nonoperating Revenues
1984	$60,000	$0	$90,000*
1985	60,000	0	90,000
1986	60,000	0	90,000
1987	60,000	0	90,000
1988	60,000	0	90,000
1989	60,000	0	90,000
1990	60,000	0	90,000
19__		—	
19__		—	*only if necessary
19__		—	

E. Inflation rates
  1. Schedule of inflation rates (round to nearest one percent):

Category	Annual Inflation Rate
a. Construction	18%
b. Equipment	8%
c. Operating and maintenance costs	7%
d. Revenues (maximum)	4%

F. Cash management
  1. Size of current unencumbered, non-designated cash surplus available to cover temporary cash deficits for the project $ 0
  2. Expected average rate of return from the investment of cash surplus over life of the project (to the nearest 1%)   9%

G. Municipal tax assessment
  1. Total property tax assessment $ 33 million
  2. Expected average annual growth rate

of the tax assessment (to the nearest 1%)   <u>2%</u>
3. Maximum tax increase the governing body will enact in support of the project's operations   <u>2 mills</u>
4. Year in which tax increase will be enacted   <u>1981</u>

H. Gifts and grants
 1. If any portion of the project is to be financed with funds other than those supplied by loans or the sale of bonds, complete the following schedule:

Schedule of Financing

(1) Year	(2) Surplus Cash	(3) Grants	(4) Other	(5) Total	(6) % of Total
19*81*	<u>0</u>	<u>0</u>	$80,000	$ 80,000	<u>40</u>%
19*82*	<u>0</u>	<u>0</u>	<u>60,000</u>	<u>60,000</u>	<u>30</u>
19*83*	<u>0</u>	<u>0</u>	<u>40,000</u>	<u>40,000</u>	<u>20</u>
19*84*	<u>0</u>	<u>0</u>	<u>20,000</u>	<u>20,000</u>	<u>10</u>
Totals				$200,000	100%

I. Debt financing
 1. At what rate of interest can long-term funds be acquired?   <u>7%</u>
 2. How will the debt be repaid?
  a. <u> x </u> out of operating revenues.
  b. <u> x </u> out of tax revenues.
 3. What is the maximum amount of debt the municipality can currently raise?   <u>5 million</u>
 4. When will the bond issue be completely retired?   <u>1990</u>
 5. When will the first sinking fund payment (loan payment) be due?   19<u>81</u>
 6. When will the proceeds of the bond issue be available?   19<u>80</u>

Supplement to Program Description Form

Part A. *Project Implementation Date:* The year in which the first cash payment is made on the project or the first cash receipts are deposited, whichever is the earlier.

Part B. *Facilities*
Lines 1a-1e: Contract price is obtainable from the bids requested by the municipality. Add to this amount the costs of any changes contemplated by the governing board. Significant changes to this cost figure because of design changes, site relocation, or other similar factors will necessitate revising the total budget. Figures should be entered without adjustment for inflation over the contract price, since this adjustment is made in Part 2 of this manual.

Lines 2a-2e: Construction progress payments are generally established as part of the contract between the municipality and the builder. The designation of first year, second year, etc., is given in Part A. The amounts in lines B2e and B1e should be equal.

Part C. *Equipment*
Lines 1a-1e: Equipment costs included here are expenditures for vehicles, furniture, tools, and so forth, that are not normally included in the facilities costs. Equipment is grouped into one classification for ease of computation; however, different equipment classifications may be used, especially if their individual inflation rates are significantly different. The timing of the payment for equipment purchases is also an important

consideration. The dollar amounts entered here are adjusted for inflation, since this calculation is performed in Part 2 of this manual.

Part D. *Operating Costs and Revenues*
The planning model covers the entire life of the operations. Operating and maintenance costs should reflect the growth in the program, where applicable. The desired surplus from operations (that will be used for purposes other than the project) should be designated as either a constant or a variable annual figure. Operating revenues, plus any other revenues designated usable by the project itself, should be equal to or greater than the sum of operating and maintenance (O and M) costs plus the desired annual surplus.

The first year of operation is generally the first year after the construction is completed. If the volume of services is expected to influence the operating budget in later years—by either increasing or decreasing costs and revenues—the figures should be adjusted to account for these volume related changes. Price and wage inflation *should not* be considered at this point. A later adjustment will be made to cover this type of cost increase. The sources of these data must necessarily evolve from the planning process that takes place at the order of the governing body. Accuracy is of critical importance here.

Part E. *Inflation Rates*
These rates should be rounded to the nearest 1% to reduce the complexity of computations.

Line 1a: Construction cost inflation may be obtained from contractors and builders in your area.

Line 1b: Equipment inflation rates may be obtained from equipment dealers, the consulting engineer, or other similar sources.

Line 1c: Operating and maintenance cost inflation is generally based on the historical experience in your municipal government or on that in nearby municipalities. If the facilities are specialized or unique in some manner, the annual O and M increases should be programmed at the rate that reflects these circumstances. The consulting engineer should be able to help with this estimate.

Line 1d: Some projects do not produce revenues, and for those that do, it may not be desirable or permissible to increase revenues over time. In other situations, the governing body may have complete control over the inflation rate.

> *Note:* Local prices and price levels are often different from the national price index figures or figures obtained from other states or regions.

Part F. *Cash Management*

Line 1: This amount should be considered as a pool of funds that can be "loaned" to the project and which will be repaid during its expected life.

Line 2: The interest rate should be rounded to the nearest 1% based on the *effective* annual rate of interest. Your banker will provide that figure. It will be different from the nominal (advertised) interest rate if the cash deposit is compounded daily, for example.

Part G. *Tax Assessment*

Line 2: The growth rate should be projected based on past experience and expected or known future property development.

Line 3: This rate must be supplied if general obligation bonds will help finance the project.

Part H. *Gifts and Grants*

The figures supplied here are estimates based on planning to this point. The planning model will confirm the sufficiency or deficiency of these plans.

> *Note:* If your project's operating costs and revenues do not fit into the pattern suggested by Schedule D, you should change the headings to suit your particular needs. In any case, do not include any overhead allocations in these figures. They should include only *incremental cash* expenditures and revenues directly attributable to the operation of the proposed project.

Part I. *Debt Financing*

Line 1: The investment banker, syndicate, or lender will provide this figure.

Line 2: Designate the source of funds that will be used to retire the indebtedness. You may select both, if you wish to test both options.

Line 3: This figure may be a legal or practical limit on municipal debt.

Lines 4-6: The lender will assist in supplying these data.

Part 2. Inflation and Interest Rate Adjustments

Definition: Inflation and interest rate adjustments are merely simple mathematic computations that adjust the figures provided in the *Program Description*.

Format: Multicolumn accounting paper

Purpose: Its purpose is to enable the financial officer to make proper allowances for (1) the effects of inflation on future budget periods as a result of implementing the project; (2) the growth rate of the tax assessment on the tax revenues available to support the project's operations; and (3) the interest effects of transferring funds into and out of the municipality's cash surplus account.

Sources of Data: The basic data are found in the *Program Description*. Compound interest and present value factors are presented in Tables A, B, and C in this manual.

CAPITAL BUDGET MANUAL/77

Schedule 1
Inflation Adjustment for Construction and Equipment Costs

	Construction Cost*	CIF @ _18%_**	(1) x (2)	Equipment Cost†	CIF @ _8%_††	(4) x (5)	Total Inflated Cost (3)+(6)
Current year 19 _80_							
Project year 1-19 _81_	$150,000	1.000	$150,000				$150,000
2-19 _82_	250,000	1.000	250,000				250,000
3-19 _83_	400,000	1.000	400,000	$100,000	1.2597	$125,970	525,970
4-19 _84_							
5-19 _85_							
6-19 _86_							
7-19 _87_							
8-19 _88_							
9-19 _89_							
10-19 _90_							

* Section B of *Program Description*
** Section E of *Program Description* (see instructions in supplement)
† Section C of *Program Description*
†† Section E of *Program Description*

Schedule 2
Inflation Adjustment for Operating and Maintenance Costs and Revenues

	O and M costs*	CIF @ 7%**	Inflated O and M costs (1) x (2)	Non-tax Revenues*	CIF @ 4½%**	Inflated Revenues (4) x (5)
Current year 19 80						
Project year 1-19 81						
2-19 82						
3-19 83						
4-19 84	$60,000	1.3108	$78,648	$90,000	1.1699	$105,291
5-19 85	60,000	1.4026	84,156	90,000	1.2167	109,503
6-19 86	60,000	1.5007	90,042	90,000	1.2653	113,877
7-19 87	60,000	1.6058	96,348	90,000	1.3159	118,431
8-19 88	60,000	1.7182	103,092	90,000	1.3686	123,174
9-19 89	60,000	1.8385	110,310	90,000	1.4233	128,097
10-19 90	60,000	1.9672	118,032	90,000	1.4802	133,218

* Section D of Program Description
** Section E of Program Description

CAPITAL BUDGET MANUAL/**79**

Schedule 3
Present Value of Inflated Costs and Revenues

		Total Inflated Costs* (1)	PVF @ 9%*** (2)	PV of Inflated Costs (1) x (2) (3)	Inflated Non-tax Revenues*** (4)	PV of Inflated Revenues (4) x (2)	PV of Net Costs (3) - (5)
Current year	19 80						
Project year	1-19 81	$150,000	.91743	$137,615			$137,615
	2-19 82	250,000	.84168	210,420			210,420
	3-19 83	525,970	.77218	406,144			406,144
	4-19 84	78,648	.70843	55,717	$105,291	$74,591	(18,874)
	5-19 85	84,156	.64993	54,696	109,503	71,169	(16,473)
	6-19 86	90,042	.59627	53,689	113,877	67,901	(14,212)
	7-19 87	96,348	.54703	52,705	118,431	64,785	(12,080)
	8-19 88	103,092	.50187	51,739	123,174	61,817	(10,078)
	9-19 89	110,310	.46043	50,790	128,097	58,980	(8,190)
	10-19 90	118,032	.42241	49,858	133,218	56,273	(6,415)
Totals			6.41766	$1,123,373		$455,516	$667,857

* Column (7), Schedule 1, plus column (3), Schedule 2. For 1981, the figures are $150,000 + $0 = $150,000.
** Section F, Line 2 of *Program Description*
*** Column (6), Schedule 2

Schedule 4
Present Value of Property Tax Revenues and Gifts and Grants

		Tax Assessment*	Prior Year's CIF @ 2%**	Tax Revenues (1) x (2) x PVF @ 9%*** (2.0 mills)†		PV of Tax Revenues (3) x (4)	Gifts and Grants	PV of Gifts and Grants (6) x (4)
Current year	19 80	33,000,000						
Project year	1-19 81		1.0000	$ 66,000	.91743	$ 60,550	$ 80,000	$ 73,394
	2-19 82		1.0200	67,320	.84168	56,662	60,000	50,501
	3-19 83		1.0404	68,666	.77218	53,023	40,000	30,887
	4-19 84		1.0612	70,039	.70843	49,618	20,000	14,169
	5-19 85		1.0824	71,438	.64993	46,430		
	6-19 86		1.1041	72,871	.59627	43,451		
	7-19 87		1.1262	74,329	.54703	40,660		
	8-19 88		1.1487	75,814	.50187	38,049		
	9-19 89		1.1717	77,332	.46043	35,606		
	10-19 90		1.1951	78,877	.42241	33,318		
				$722,686		$457,367		$168,951

* Section G of *Program Description*
** Section F of *Program Description*
† Section H of *Program Description*

Supplement to Inflation and Interest Rate Adjustment

Schedule 1. If construction begins in project year 1, no inflation adjustment is required for construction costs. The dollar figures found in Section B2 can be placed directly in column (3). If construction is delayed, the *CIF* used to adjust each year's construction cost will be that for the year in which construction begins.

Inflation rates used are those given in Section E of the *Program Description*; the *CIFs* for various inflation rates and future years are found in Table A located at the end of this manual.

Schedule 2. Operations begin after construction is completed and equipment is installed. The use of the *CIFs* are the same as described earlier. The cash flow data are found in Section D of the *Program Description*, and the inflation rates are those given in Section E.

Schedule 3. Column (1) figures are obtained from columns (7) and (3) in Schedules 1 and 2, respectively. These figures are multiplied by the Present Value Factors (*PVFs*) for the rate of interest earned on cash surpluses (Section F, line 2). The *PVFs* are found in Table C. Columns (3), (5), and (6) are totaled.

Schedule 4. The municipality's tax assessment, its growth rate, and the maximum millage rate increase are obtained from Section G in the *Program Description*. Column (2) contains the compound interest factors (*CIF*) for the growth rate of the tax assessment. The *CIF* are lagged one year, since this year's tax revenues are based on last year's tax assessment. Column (3) contains the nominal dollar tax revenues expected in each year from project year 1 as a result of the tax increase permitted in Section G of the *Program Description*. Column (5) should be totaled giving the present value of total tax revenues for the life of the project, discounted at the interest rate earned on surplus cash.

Column (6) contains the other sources of funds listed in Part H of the *Program Description*. The dollar amounts are discounted at the rate earned on surplus cash, and column (7) is totaled.

Part 3. Financial Viability Tests

Definition: Four tests for financial viability are included in this part of the manual—one for each of the four financing options.

Format: Multicolumn accounting forms and decision forms.

Purpose: The purpose of the tests for financial viability is to assure that the project will be financially self-supporting out of revenues and funds from any of the four financing options (or combinations thereof).

Sources of Data: The data are found in the *Program Description* and the schedules contained in Part 2 of this manual.

Section A. Gifts and Grants Option

Definition: This section provides a test for financial viability when a project is to be funded by gifts and grants whose payments extend over two or more years.

Format: Multicolumn accounting paper and decision forms.

Purpose: The purpose of this step is to calculate the amount of money needed to construct, equip, and operate the project outlined in the *Program Description*, given that the sole funding source is gifts and grants. If the funds provided under this option are inadequate to achieve project financial viability, one or more of four alternatives must be selected:
  1. Abandon the project
  2. Scale down the project
  3. Increase the rate at which funds are collected
  4. Search for other sources of funds

Using alternatives 2 and/or 4, the budget analyst must redefine the problem and make the necessary changes in the *Program Description* and recompute Schedules 1 through 4.

If the funds available from gifts and grants are more than adequate to finance the project, the excess can be applied elsewhere.

Sources of Data: The data are provided in the *Program Description*, Part H, and in Schedule 3.

Schedule 5
Calculation of Present Value Factor, f

	Distribution of Gifts and Grants*	PVF @ 9%**	Present Value of Distribution (1) × (2)
Current year 19 80	—	1.0000	
Project year 1-19 81	.40	.91743	.36697
2-19 82	.30	.84168	.25250
3-19 83	.20	.77218	.15444
4-19 84	.10	.70843	.07084
5-19 85			
6-19 86			
7-19 87			
8-19 88			
9-19 89			
10-19 90			
Totals	1.00		f = .84475

* Section H, column (6), of *Program Description*. Enter figures in decimals.
** Section F of *Program Description*. Factors are found in Table C.

Schedule 6

Calculation of Nominal Dollar Amount of Gifts and Grants Needed to Fund the Project

1. Present value of net project costs
   (total of column (6), Schedule 3) $ 667,857

2. Present value factor, f (total of
   column (3), Schedule 5)   .84475

3. Divide figure in line 1 by figure in line 2 $ 790,597

4. Total funds expected from gifts and
   grants (total of column (5), Section H
   of *Program Description*)   200,000

5. Line 3 minus line 4 $ 590,597

If the figure in line 5 is greater than zero:
 Your project is underfunded by this amount as of the current date. You should be prepared to commit that amount out of your cash surplus to this project, OR plan to raise the funds from other sources (see other options), OR scale down the project (begin over), OR abandon the project (stop).

If the figure in line 5 is zero (plus or minus $200 or $300):
 Funding from gifts and grants is almost exactly sufficient to implement the project and operate for its specified life.

If the figure in line 5 is less than zero (by a significant amount):

You have overfunded the project. You may reduce the fund-raising goal by the amount in line 5 or plan other uses for the surplus funds.

Supplement to Gifts and Grants Option

Schedule 5. The percentage distribution of gifts and grants is taken from the *Program Description*, Section H, column (6), and should be entered in decimal form. The total of column (1) in this schedule should be equal to 1.00. The present value factor, f, which is the total of the figures in column (3) is entered in line 2 of Schedule 6.

Schedule 6. The decision point is line 5. When the figure in line 5 is greater than zero, you must select one or more of the following alternatives regarding the project.

1. *Scale down the project.* This requires complete replanning. The *Program Description* must be rewritten, and Schedules 1 through 6 must be revised so that line 5 becomes equal to or less than zero.

2. *Raise more money.* The figure in line 5 is the nominal amount that is to be added to the fund-raising goal and collected in the proportions specified in the *Program Description*. If the additional money will be received in a lump sum in the current year, the dollar amount required is calculated by

multiplying line 5 by line 2 to reduce the figure to a present-value amount.

The budget analyst may also examine the other financing options when line 5 is greater than zero.

3. *Use your cash surplus.* This alternative merely requires that you encumber and transfer the present value of the amount in line 5 to the project fund. This transfer must be accomplished immediately, so that it may begin earning interest for the project.

These alternatives are not mutually exclusive; however, if line 5 remains greater than zero after you have made all the adjustments possible, the project should be abandoned to prevent future financial crises from developing.

Section B. Tax Increase Option

Definition: This is a decision point in the long-range planning model when the project is to be funded at least partially with tax revenues. The total funding requirements are determined at this point, and the tax increase option is examined for financial viability.

Format: Decision form.

Purpose: The purpose of this step is to calculate the amount of money needed to construct, equip, and operate the project outlined in the *Program Description*. If the funds requirement is too large, one of three alternatives must be selected:
1. Abandon the project
2. Scale down the project
3. Search for other sources of funds

Using alternatives 2 and 3, the budget analyst must redefine the problem and make the necessary changes in the *Program Description* and recompute Schedules 1, 2, 3, and 4.

If the funds promised are more than adequate, the tax increase may be adjusted downward.

Sources of Data: The data are found in the *Program Description*, Part H, and in Schedules 3 and 4.

Schedule 7

Calculation of Funding Requirements

1. Present value of inflation-adjusted net costs (total of column (6), Schedule 3) $ _667,857_

2. Present values of tax revenues (total of column (5), Schedule 4)   _457,367_

3. Line 1 minus line 2 (if zero or less, the tax increase is too large. See instructions below) $ _210,490_

4. Present value of gifts and grants (total of column (7), Schedule 4)   _168,951_

5. Line 3 minus line 4 $ _41,539_

If the figure in line 5 is greater than zero:
  Your project is underfunded by this much as of the current date. You should be prepared to commit that amount out of your cash surplus to this project, OR plan to raise the amount from other sources, OR plan to increase the tax rate by a greater amount than currently planned (continue with line 6 below), OR scale down the project (begin over), OR abandon the project (stop).

If the figure in line 5 is zero (plus or minus $200 or $300):
  Your funding is almost exactly sufficient to implement the project and operate it for the specified life of the project (skip the remainder of this schedule, and go to the next part of the manual).

If the figure in line 3 or line 5 is less than zero:
  You have overfunded the project. You may reduce the

tax rate increase or plan other uses for the surplus amount shown in line 5.

If the absolute (disregarding the sign) value of line 5 is greater than that of line 2, no tax increase at all will be required. If the absolute value of line 5 is less than that of line 2, continue with line 6 below.

6. Enter figure from line 1 above $ _667,857_

7. Enter figure from line 4   _168,951_

8. Line 6 minus line 7   = $ _498,906_

9. Divide amount in line 8 by the amount in line 2   =   _1.0908_

10. Enter the millage rate increase (Section G, line 3, of the *Program Description*)   _2.0_ mills

11. Multiply line 9 by line 10   =   _2.182_ mills

The figure in line 11 is the approximate millage rate increase needed to fund the project. This tax increase is in addition to the funds available from gifts and grants and operating revenues.

Supplement to Tax Increase Option

Line 7:   This is the decision point.
If the figure in line 5 is greater than zero, you must select one of the following options regarding the project.

1. *Scale down the project.* This requires complete replanning. The *Program Description* must be completely rewritten since most projects are not completely divisible.

2. *Raise more money.* The figure in line 5 is the amount needed right *now*, since it is a present value figure. If you plan to receive the money in one or more years from now, the amount you must ask for is the amount in line 7 times the appropriate *CIF* from Table A. For example, if line 5 is equal to $116,852, you would get the money in two years, and if the interest rate on the cash surplus is 7%, the amount of money you must receive in two years is

$$\$116{,}852 \times 1.1449 = \$133{,}784.$$

The *CIF*, 1.1449, is found in Table A, in the 7% column at year 2.

3. *Use your cash surplus.* This alternative merely requires you to encumber and transfer the amount in line 7 to the project fund. The transfer must be accomplished immediately, so that it may begin earning interest for the project.

4. *Raise taxes by a greater amount than planned in the Program Description.* The specific tax increase is given in line 11 of this Schedule. Alternatives 2, 3, and 4 above require that Schedule 4 be recalculated and the revised figures substituted into Schedule 5.

Section C. Revenue Bond Option

Definition: This is a decision point in the long-range planning model when the project is to be financed at least in part with revenue bonds (or a loan, the repayment of which will come from excess revenues over operating costs). The revenue bond option is examined for financial viability and the amount is calculated by which annual revenues are excessive or insufficient to support the bond issue.

Format: Decision form.

Purpose: The purpose of this section is to calculate the maximum size of a revenue bond issue that can be repaid out of nontax revenues. This figure is then compared with the amount of money needed to fully finance the project; i.e., construct, equip, and operate it over its expected life.

If the bond issue size is larger than needed, the decision form will indicate the amount by which annual revenues may be reduced (or diverted to other uses). Similarly, if the bond issue is too small, the decision form will indicate the amount by which annual nontax revenues will have to be increased to make the project financially viable.

Sources of Data: The data are found in the *Program Description*, Parts F and I, and in Schedules 1, 3, and 4.

Schedule 8

Compound Interest Calculations

The purpose of these calculations is to provide input data for use in Schedule 9.

1. Number of years from current year until the bond issue matures (*Program Description*, Section I) $s =$ __10__ years

2. Maturity of the bond issue in years (*Program Description*, Section I) $m =$ __10__ years

3. Bond interest rate as a decimal (*Program Description*, Section I) $b =$ __.07__

4. Expected average rate of return from invested cash surplus as a decimal (*Program Description*, Section F) $r =$ __.09__

5. Present Value Factor (*PVF*) at b (line 3) for m (line 2) years (Table C)   __.50835__

6. Subtract the amount in line 5 from 1.00000 $=$ __.49165__

7. Divide the amount in line 6 by b in line 3 $=$ __7.02357__

8. Present Value Factor (*PVF*) at r (line 4) for s (line 1) years (Table C)   __.42241__

9. Subtract the amount in line 8
   from 1.0000   =   .57759

10. Divide *r* in line 4 by the
    amount in line 9   =   .15582

11. Multiply the amount in line 7
    by the amount in line 10, and
    enter the result in Schedule 9,
    line 6.   =   *1.09441*

Schedule 9

Calculation of Revenue Bond Issue Size and Amount of Operating Surplus (Deficit)

Enter amount from column (7), Schedule 1, in the table below.

Year	Amount from Col. (7), Sched. 1	PVF @ 9 %*	PV of Const. & Equip. Costs
1981	$150,000	.91743	$137,615
1982	250,000	.84168	210,420
1983	525,970	.77218	406,144
Totals		2.53129	$754,179

* Section F of *Program Description*. Figures are found in Table C.

1. Present value of construction and equipment costs (total of column (4) from table above) $ 754,179

2. Present value of gifts and grants (total of column (7), Schedule 4) $ 168,951

3. Line 1 minus line 2   = $ 585,228

4. Present value of net costs (total of column (6), Schedule 3)   667,857

5. Line 4 minus line 3   = $ 82,629

6. Enter figure from line 11,
   Schedule 8   *1.09441*

7. Multiply the amount on line
   5 by line 6   = $ *90,430*

The figure in line 7 is the maximum revenue bond issue size that can be amortized out of the project's net revenues.

8. Enter the total of column (2),
   Schedule 3   *6.41766*

9. Enter the total of column (3)
   from the table above   *2.53129*

10. Line 8 minus line 9   =   *3.88637*

11. Add lines 2 and 7   = $ *259,381*

12. Line 11 minus line 5   = $ *176,752*

13. Line 4 minus line 12   = $ *491,105*

14. Divide amount in line 13
    by line 10   = $ *126,366*

The figure in line 14, if greater than zero, is the amount by which annual revenues must be increased to achieve project financial viability. If less than zero, it is the annual surplus the project will generate once operations begin.

Supplement to Revenue Bond Option

Schedule 8. This is designed to facilitate the computation of a complex present value factor that is used to calculate the maximum size of the revenue bond issue. The present value factors used in lines 5 and 8 are found in Table C.

Schedule 9.
Line 7 The figure in line 7 is the maximum bond issue size that can be amortized out of the excess of cash inflows less operating costs. In order for the project to be totally viable, the bond issue size must be equal to or greater than the present value of construction and equipment costs. If it is not, the operating revenues must be increased by an amount indicated on line 14 to achieve financial viability.

Line 14 This is the decision point. Line 14 indicates whether the project will generate surplus revenues or produce a deficit in cash flows, and the governing body will have to decide how best to dispose of the surplus funds or overcome the deficit.

Section D. General Obligation Bond Option

Definition: This section provides a test for financial viability when a project is to be funded by a general obligation bond issue (or intermediate-term loan to be repaid out of property tax revenues).

Format: Decision form.

Purpose: The purpose of this section is to calculate the maximum size of a general obligation bond issue that can be repaid out of a property tax increase of specified number of mills. This figure is then compared with the amount of money needed to construct, equip, and operate the project over its expected life.

The decision form will indicate the size of the bond issue required and the millage rate needed to repay the principal and interest in equal annual payments over its maturity. If the millage rate is in excess of that rate allowed by the governing authority, the decision form will calculate the maximum size of the bond issue supportable out of the maximum millage rate increase allowed.

Sources of Data: Data are found in the *Program Description*, Parts F, G, and I, and in Schedules 1, 3, 4, and 5.

Schedule 10

Compound Interest Calculations

The purpose of these calculations is to provide input data for use in Schedule 11.

1. Number of years from current year until the bond issue matures (*Program Description*, Section I) $s =$ _10_ years

2. Maturity of the bond issue in years (*Program Description*, Section I) $m =$ _10_ years

3. Bond interest rate as a decimal (*Program Description*, Section I) $b =$ _.07_

4. Expected average rate of return from invested cash surplus as a decimal (*Program Description*, Section F) $r =$ _.09_

5. Present value factor (*PVF*) at b (line 3) for m (line 2) years (Table C)   _.50835_

6. Subtract the amount in line 5 from 1.00000 $=$ _.49165_

7. Divide b in line 3 by amount in line 6 $=$ _.14238_

8. Present value factor (*PVF*) at r (line 4) for s (line 1) years (Table C)   _.42241_

9. Subtract the amount in line 8
   from 1.00000   =   .57759

10. Divide amount in line 9 by r
    in line 4   = 6.41767

11. Multiply the amount in line 7
    by the amount in line 10, and
    enter the result in Schedule 11,
    line 7   = 0.91375

Schedule 11

Calculation of General Obligation Bond Size and Millage Rate Increase Required

Enter amounts from Schedule 1, column (7), in the table below.

* Section F of *Program Description*.

1. Enter total amount of column (4) from table above $ __754,179__

2. Present value of gifts and grants (total of column (7), Schedule 4) $ __168,951__

3. Line 1 minus line 2 (if zero or less, additional financing is not required)   =$ __585,228__

The amount in line 3 is the present value of the inflation-adjusted construction and equipment costs after deducting the present value of gifts and grants.

4. Enter total amount of column (6), Schedule 3   __667,857__

5. Subtract line 4 from line 1   =$ __86,322__

6. Line 3 minus line 5   =$ __498,906__

If the amount in line 6 is greater than zero, the figure represents the size of the bond issue needed to finance the project. If it is zero or less, the project's revenues are sufficient to finance the project and no bond issue is required. The amount of line 6, if less than zero, is equal to the present value of surplus funds that may be reallocated to other uses.

7. Enter the amount from line 11,
   Schedule 10   .91375

8. Multiply amount in line 6 by
   amount in line 7   = $ 455,875

9. Enter total of column (5)
   Schedule 4   = $ 457,367

10. Enter the figure in line 3,
    Section G of *Program
    Description*, in decimals   .002

11. Divide amount in line 9 by
    amount in line 10   = $228,683,500

12. Divide amount in line 8
    by amount in line 11   =   .001993

The figure in line 12 is the approximate millage rate needed to repay the bond principal (plus interest) that will completely finance the project. If this rate is greater than the maximum allowable rate specified in Section G of the *Program Description*, you will have to scale down the project or obtain additional financing. The amount of additional financing is calculated below:

13. Enter the amount from
    line 9 above $ 457,367

14. Enter the amount from line
    7 above   .91375

15. Divide amount in line
    13 by amount in line 14   = $ 500,538

The figure in line 15 is the maximum size of the bond issue that the tax revenues at the maximum allowable millage rate will service (i.e., repay principal plus interest in equal annual payments).

16. Subtract amount in line
    15 from amount in line 6   = $ (1,632)

The amount in line 16, if greater than zero, is the present value of the additional financing required to make the project financially viable, or the present value of the amount by which the project must be scaled down to make it financially viable with the tax increase specified in the *Program Description*. If negative, the amount in line 16 is the present value of surplus revenues the project will generate over the planning period.

Supplement to
General Obligation Bond Option

Schedule 10. This is designed to facilitate the computation of a complex present-value factor that is used to calculate the maximum size of the general obligation bond issue. The present value factors used in lines 5 and 8 are found in Table C.

Schedule 11.
Line 6 This is the first decision point. If positive, the figure in line 6 is the size of the bond issue required to construct, equip, and operate the project over the planning period, given the data supplied in the *Program Description*. If the figure is negative, no bonds are required since the project is financially viable as planned.

Line 12 This is the second decision point. Line 12 gives the millage rate required to amortize a bond issue (of the size given in line 6) in equal annual payments. If this rate is greater than the maximum allowable millage rate, the project must be scaled down or additional funding should be sought to complete the financing package. The amount involved in either alternative is given in line 16.

Line 16 This is the third decision point. If the figure is positive, the maximum millage rate increase specified in the *Program Description* is too small to achieve project financial viability under this option. In this case the project should be scaled down by the amount in line 16 (on a present-value basis) or additional financing must be acquired in that amount (also on a present-value basis). Failing this, the project must be abandoned in order to avoid future financial crises. A negative figure represents a cash flow surplus (on a present-value basis) that can be diverted to other uses.

Part 4. Project Cash-Flow Characteristics*

Definition: Project cash-flow characteristics are revealed by organizing in tabular form the dollar inflows and outflows created by the implementation and subsequent operation of the project.

Format: Multicolumn accounting paper.

Purpose: By netting out the cash inflows and outflows, the budget analyst is able to predict when cash deficits and surpluses will occur over the life of the project. This will aid in managing the surplus cash accounts and signal the need for short-term borrowing to cover temporary deficits.

Sources of Data: The basic data are drawn from Schedules 3 and 4 and the *Program Description*. Additionally, the schedules contained in Parts A through D in Part 3 supply other necessary data.

---

* Each option presented in Part 3 of this manual will produce a different cash flow for any given project; therefore, four cash-flow schedules—one for each option—are presented here. The assumption that the municipal governing body is able to modify the program to achieve financial viability under each option is adopted in order to complete the illustration.

CAPITAL BUDGET MANUAL/107

Schedule 12A
Project Cash Flows Under the Gifts and Grants Option
(Viability Achieved by Increasing the Amount of Gifts Received)

	Total Inflated Costs*	Operating Revenues**	Gifts and Grants†	Net Cash Flow (2)+(3)−(1)	Beginning Cash Balance	Interest Earned(Paid) (5) × 9%††	Ending Cash Balance (4)+(5)+(6)
Current year 19 80	—	—	0	0	0	0	0
Project year 1-19 81	$150,000	0	$316,239	$166,239	0	0	$166,239
2-19 82	150,000	0	237,179	(1,282)	$166,239	$14,962	168,380
3-19 83	525,970	0	158,119	(367,851)	168,380	15,154	(184,317)
4-19 84	78,648	$105,291	79,060	105,703	(184,317)	(16,589)	(95,203)
5-19 85	84,156	109,503	0	25,347	(95,203)	(8,568)	(78,424)
6-19 86	90,042	113,877	0	23,835	(78,424)	(7,058)	(61,647)
7-19 87	96,348	118,431	0	22,083	(61,647)	(5,548)	(45,112)
8-19 88	103,092	123,174	0	20,082	(45,112)	(4,060)	(29,090)
9-19 89	110,310	128,097	0	17,787	(29,090)	(2,618)	(13,921)
10-19 90	118,032	133,218	0	15,186	(13,921)	(1,253)	12

* Column (1), Schedule 3
** Column (4), Schedule 3
† Column (6), Schedule 4, plus the amount in line 5, Schedule 6, collected in the proportions specified in Part H of the *Program Description*. For 1981, the figures are $80,000 + ($590,597 × .40) = $316,239. The addition of the funds from Schedule 6 is for the purpose of making the project viable by increasing the fund-raising goal by $590,597.
†† Part F of *Program Description*

Schedule 12B
Project Cash Flows Under the Tax Increase Option
(Viability Achieved by Increasing the Millage Rate by 2.182 Mills)

		Total Inflated Costs*	Tax Revenues**	Gifts,Grants & Operating Revenues†	Net Cash Flow (2)+(3)-(1)	Beginning Cash Balance	Interest Earned(Paid) (5) × %††	Ending Cash Balance (4)+(5)+(6)
Current year	19 80	—	—	0	0	0	0	0
Project year	1-19 81	$150,000	$72,006	$80,000	$2,006	0	0	$2,006
	2-19 82	252,000	73,446	60,000	(118,557)	$2,006	$181	(116,367)
	3-19 83	525,970	74,915	40,000	(411,055)	(116,367)	(10,293)	(535,715)
	4-19 84	78,678	74,715	125,291	123,056	(535,715)	(48,214)	(460,873)
	5-19 85	84,150	77,939	109,503	103,286	(460,873)	(41,479)	(399,066)
	6-19 86	90,042	79,502	113,877	103,337	(399,066)	(35,916)	(331,645)
	7-19 87	96,346	80,095	118,431	103,176	(331,645)	(29,848)	(258,317)
	8-19 88	103,092	82,713	123,174	102,795	(258,317)	(23,249)	(178,771)
	9-19 89	110,310	84,369	128,097	102,156	(178,771)	(16,089)	(92,704)
	10-19 90	118,032	86,054	133,218	101,240	(92,704)	(8,343)	193

* Column (1), Schedule 3

** Schedule 4 (column (1) × column (2) × 2.182 mills). For 1981, the figures are $33,000,000 × 1.000 × .002182 = $72,006. The additional 2.182 mills is included to make the project viable by allowing the millage rate to increase by 4.182 mills.

† Column (4), Schedule 3, plus column (6), Schedule 4. For 1984, the figures are $105,291 + $20,000 = $125,291.

†† Part F of *Program Description*

Schedule 12C
Project Cash Flows Under the Revenue Bond Option
(Viability Achieved by Increasing Small Operating Revenues by $126,366 in project years 4-10)

		Total Inflated Costs*	Gifts, Grants & Operating Revenues**	Debt Service Charges†	Net Cash Flow (2)-(1)-(3)	Beginning Cash Balance	Interest Earned(Paid) (5) × 9%††	Ending Cash Balance (4)+(5)+(6)
Current year	19 80				0	0	0	$ 90,430
Project year	1-19 81	$150,000	$ 80,000	$ 12,875	$ (82,875)	$ 90,430	8,139	15,694
	2-19 82	250,000	60,000	12,875	(202,875)	15,694	1,412	(185,769)
	3-19 83	525,970	40,000	12,875	(498,845)	(185,769)	(16,717)	(701,333)
	4-19 84	78,648	251,657	12,875	160,134	(701,333)	(63,120)	(604,319)
	5-19 85	84,156	255,869	12,875	158,838	(604,319)	(54,387)	(519,870)
	6-19 86	90,042	240,243	12,875	137,326	(519,870)	(46,788)	(429,332)
	7-19 87	96,348	244,797	12,875	135,574	(429,332)	(38,640)	(332,398)
	8-19 88	103,092	249,540	12,875	133,573	(332,398)	(29,916)	(228,741)
	9-19 89	110,310	254,463	12,875	131,278	(228,741)	(20,587)	(118,050)
	10-19 90	118,032	259,584	12,875	128,677	(118,050)	(10,625)	2

* Column (1), Schedule 3
** Column (4). Schedule 3, plus column (6), Schedule 4, plus $126,366 in years 4-10. For 1984, the figures are $105,291 + $20,000 + $126,366 = $251,657. The $126,366 is the added operating revenues needed to repay the revenue bonds. That figure is found in line 14 of Schedule 9.
† Line 7, Schedule 9, divided by line 7, Schedule 8. The figures are $90,430/7.02357 = $12,875.
†† Part F of *Program Description*

Schedule 12D
Project Cash Flows Under the General Bond Option

		Total Inflated Costs*	Debt Service Charges**	Total Cash Inflows†	Net Cash Flow (3)−(2)−(1)	Beginning Cash Balance	Interest Earned(Paid) (5) × 9%††	Ending Cash Balance (4)+(5)+(6)
Current year	19 80							
Project year	1-19 81	$150,000	$71,034	$145,767	(75,267)	0	0	$498,906
	2-19 82	250,000	71,034	127,084	(193,950)	$498,906	$44,902	468,543
	3-19 83	525,970	71,034	108,426	(488,578)	468,543	42,169	316,762
	4-19 84	78,678	71,034	195,085	45,403	316,762	28,507	193,307
	5-19 85	84,156	71,034	180,691	25,501	(143,307)	(12,898)	(1,860)
	6-19 86	90,042	71,074	186,493	25,417	(110,802)	(9,972)	(95,273)
	7-19 87	96,348	71,034	192,500	25,118	(95,273)	(8,575)	(78,451)
	8-19 88	103,092	71,034	198,723	24,597	(78,453)	(7,059)	(60,372)
	9-19 89	110,310	71,034	205,159	23,815	(60,372)	(5,433)	(41,208)
	10-19 90	118,032	71,034	218,118	22,762	(41,208)	(3,707)	(21,402)
						(21,402)	(1,899)	(249)

* Column (1), Schedule 3
** Line 6, Schedule 11, times line 7, Schedule 10. The figures are $498,906 × .14238 = $71,034.
† Schedule 4 (Column (1) × Column (2) × line 12, Schedule 11), plus Column (4), Schedule 3, plus Column (6), Schedule 4. The figures for 1984 are ($33,000,000 × 1.0612 × .001993) + $105,291 + $20,000 = $195,085. These figures represent tax revenues, operating revenues, and donations, respectively.
†† Part F of *Program Description*

Part 5. Project Controls

Definition: Project controls are mechanisms designed to monitor actual performance from project implementation through the final year of planned operation.

Format: Multicolumn accounting paper.

Purpose: One thing is certain about project planning: The plans we make are going to be wrong. Because we know that, we must prevent "being wrong" from turning into disaster. Thus, we establish a control system that will let us know the following:

      1. Why we were wrong
      2. By how much we were wrong
      3. What we must do about it

Armed with this information, we can benefit from the fact that we know that our plans are less than completely accurate and thus we must keep on top of things by controlling the project.

Sources of Data: It will be helpful if accounting records are kept on a project basis. In that way, actual project costs can be conveniently reported. The forms in the manual provide the data needed to control all aspects of the project, from the estimates recorded in the *Program Description* to the cash balance forecasted in Schedules 12A through 12D.

Supplement to Cash-Flow Characteristics

Columns 1, 2, & 3 The figures in these columns are the forecasted dollar amounts that will be spent by the municipality in support of the project, received as incremental tax revenues from the millage rate increase, and received as operating revenues and/or raised from other sources. Each of these figures represents the future cash deposits and future cash expenditures on behalf of the project.

Column 4 This column presents the difference between cash receipts and cash expenditures over the life of the project.

Columns 5 & 7 The ending cash balance in any one year (column 7) is the beginning cash balance for the following year (column 5).

Column 6 These figures are the interest earned (lost) on the cash surpluses (deficits) generated by the project in each period, calculated at the rate earned on surplus cash.

> Note: The final figure in column (7) should approximate zero. Because of rounding errors in both the computations that precede this schedule and those completed in the schedule, the figure will generally range around zero by ± $300.

Guidelines to Control

Timing: Project revenue and expense reports should be prepared and analyzed monthly; however, quarterly reports are generally satisfactory. Reports prepared less frequently than four times per year are almost always inadequate for control purposes.

Format: Each revenue or expense account should be recorded as follows:

Revenue or Expense Item	Current Month (Quarter)			Year to date			Fiscal Year Unexpended Balance
	Budget	Actual	Variance Budget-Actual	Budget	Actual	Variance Budget-Actual	
$	$	$		$	$	$	$

Accounts: The accounts used in the control process will depend on the nature of the project. For the zoological park, these accounts should be followed:

Account	Source of Budget Data
Construction costs	Schedule 1
Equipment costs	1
Operating costs	2
Gifts and grants	4
Operating revenues	3
Tax assessment	4
Tax revenues	4
Total inflated costs	3
Net cash flow	12
Cash balance	12

Analysis: Any variance of actual *over* budget in an expense item and actual *under* budget in a revenue item will create a net cash drain on the total resources of the municipality, unless it is offset by an opposite variance in another account. The budget analyst is not so much concerned with trying to balance cash outflows and inflows created by budget variances as he is with determining the *causes* of such variances and seeking ways to *correct* them or *accommodate* them (if they cannot or should not be corrected).

For example, suppose that the decision was made to pay a higher salary than budgeted to a resident veterinarian that the city felt was top notch. This would create an "unfavorable" variance in the personnel account, but from a quality point of view, the zoo's operations would benefit. Thus, we would not want to correct the variance, but accommodate it instead by reallocating funds from other sources, if possible.

Similarly, each variance of significant proportions would have to be examined and its cause determined after each reporting period. If the revenues and expenses were getting totally "out of control" and the operations could not be changed to correct the situation, the entire project should be reexamined; that is, submitted to another capital budget analysis.

Reprogramming:

When reanalysis, or reprogramming, is deemed appropriate, the project should be examined as an "operating entity" only. All past costs are to be ignored. The question becomes, "How much more in taxes or community contributions is needed to keep this project financially viable?" The answer to this question is readily obtained by beginning again with the *Program Description* and working through to Schedule 12 under the financing option selected.

Table A: Amount to which $1 will accumulate

Period	1%	2%	3%	4%	5%	6%	7%	8%	9%	10%	12%	14%	15%	16%	18%	20%	24%	28%	32%	36%
1	1.0100	1.0200	1.0300	1.0400	1.0500	1.0600	1.0700	1.0800	1.0900	1.1000	1.1200	1.1400	1.1500	1.1600	1.1800	1.2000	1.2400	1.2800	1.3200	1.3600
2	1.0201	1.0404	1.0609	1.0816	1.1025	1.1236	1.1449	1.1664	1.1881	1.2100	1.2544	1.2996	1.3225	1.3456	1.3924	1.4400	1.5376	1.6384	1.7424	1.8496
3	1.0303	1.0612	1.0927	1.1249	1.1576	1.1910	1.2250	1.2597	1.2950	1.3310	1.4049	1.4815	1.5209	1.5609	1.6430	1.7280	1.9066	1.9972	2.3000	2.5155
4	1.0406	1.0824	1.1255	1.1699	1.2155	1.2625	1.3108	1.3605	1.4116	1.4641	1.5735	1.6890	1.7490	1.8106	1.9388	2.0736	2.3642	2.6844	3.0360	3.4210
5	1.0510	1.1041	1.1593	1.2167	1.2763	1.3382	1.4026	1.4693	1.5386	1.6105	1.7623	1.9254	2.0114	2.1003	2.2878	2.4883	2.9316	3.4360	4.0075	4.6526
6	1.0615	1.1262	1.1941	1.2653	1.3401	1.4185	1.5007	1.5869	1.6771	1.7716	1.9738	2.1950	2.3131	2.4364	2.6996	2.9860	3.6352	3.9980	5.2899	6.3275
7	1.0721	1.1487	1.2299	1.3159	1.4071	1.5036	1.6058	1.7138	1.8280	1.9487	2.2107	2.5023	2.6600	2.8262	3.1855	3.5832	4.5077	5.6295	6.9826	8.6054
8	1.0829	1.1717	1.2668	1.3686	1.4775	1.5938	1.7182	1.8509	1.9926	2.1436	2.4760	2.8526	3.0590	3.2784	3.7589	4.2998	5.5895	7.2058	9.2170	11.703
9	1.0937	1.1951	1.3048	1.4233	1.5513	1.6895	1.8385	1.9990	2.1719	2.3579	2.7731	3.2519	3.5179	3.8030	4.4355	5.1598	6.9310	9.2234	12.166	15.917
10	1.1046	1.2190	1.3439	1.4802	1.6289	1.7908	1.9672	2.1589	2.3674	2.5937	3.1058	3.7072	4.0456	4.4114	5.2338	6.1917	8.5944	11.806	16.060	21.647
11	1.1157	1.2434	1.3842	1.5395	1.7103	1.8983	2.1049	2.3316	2.5804	2.8531	3.4785	4.2262	4.6524	5.1173	6.1759	7.4301	10.657	15.112	21.199	29.439
12	1.1268	1.2682	1.4258	1.6010	1.7959	2.0122	2.2522	2.5182	2.8127	3.1384	3.8960	4.8179	5.3503	5.9360	7.2876	8.9161	13.215	19.343	27.983	40.037
13	1.1381	1.2936	1.4685	1.6651	1.8856	2.1329	2.4098	2.7196	3.0658	3.4523	4.3635	5.4924	6.1528	6.8858	8.5994	10.699	16.386	24.759	36.937	54.451
14	1.1495	1.3195	1.5126	1.7317	1.9799	2.2609	2.5785	2.9372	3.3417	3.7975	4.8871	6.2613	7.0757	7.9875	10.147	12.839	20.319	31.691	48.757	74.053
15	1.1610	1.3459	1.5580	1.8009	2.0789	2.3966	2.7590	3.1722	3.6425	4.1772	5.4736	7.1379	8.1371	9.2655	11.974	15.407	25.196	40.565	64.359	100.71
16	1.1726	1.3728	1.6047	1.8730	2.1829	2.5404	2.9522	3.4259	3.9703	4.5950	6.1304	8.1372	9.3576	10.748	14.129	18.488	31.243	51.923	84.954	136.97
17	1.1843	1.4002	1.6528	1.9479	2.2920	2.6928	3.1588	3.7000	4.3276	5.0545	6.8660	9.2765	10.761	12.468	16.672	22.186	38.741	66.461	112.14	186.28
18	1.1961	1.4282	1.7024	2.0258	2.4066	2.8543	3.3799	3.9960	4.7171	5.5599	7.6900	10.575	12.375	14.463	19.673	26.623	48.039	85.071	148.02	253.34
19	1.2081	1.4568	1.7535	2.1068	2.5270	3.0256	3.6165	4.3157	5.1417	6.1159	8.6128	12.056	14.232	16.777	23.214	31.948	59.568	108.89	195.39	344.54
20	1.2202	1.4859	1.8061	2.1911	2.6533	3.2071	3.8697	4.6610	5.6044	6.7275	9.6463	13.743	16.367	19.461	27.393	38.338	73.864	139.38	257.92	468.57
21	1.2324	1.5157	1.8603	2.2788	2.7860	3.3996	4.1406	5.0338	6.1088	7.4002	10.804	15.668	18.822	22.574	32.324	46.005	91.592	178.41	340.45	637.26
22	1.2447	1.5460	1.9161	2.3699	2.9253	3.6035	4.4304	5.4365	6.6586	8.1403	12.100	17.861	21.645	26.186	38.142	55.206	113.57	228.36	449.39	866.67
23	1.2572	1.5769	1.9736	2.4647	3.0715	3.8197	4.7405	5.8715	7.2579	8.9543	13.552	20.362	24.891	30.376	45.008	66.247	140.83	292.30	593.20	1178.7
24	1.2697	1.6084	2.0328	2.5633	3.2251	4.0489	5.0724	6.3412	7.9111	9.8497	15.179	23.212	28.625	35.236	53.109	79.497	174.63	374.14	783.02	1603.0
25	1.2824	1.6406	2.0938	2.6658	3.3864	4.2919	5.4274	6.8485	8.6231	10.835	17.000	26.462	32.919	40.874	62.669	95.396	216.54	478.90	1033.6	2180.1
26	1.2953	1.6734	2.1566	2.7725	3.5557	4.5494	5.8074	7.3964	9.3992	11.918	19.040	30.167	37.857	47.414	73.949	114.48	268.51	613.00	1364.3	2964.9
27	1.3082	1.7069	2.2213	2.8834	3.7335	4.8223	6.2139	7.9881	10.245	13.110	21.325	34.390	43.535	55.000	87.260	137.37	332.95	784.64	1800.9	4032.3
28	1.3213	1.7410	2.2879	2.9987	3.9201	5.1117	6.6488	8.6271	11.167	14.421	23.884	39.204	50.066	63.800	102.97	164.84	412.86	1004.3	2377.2	5483.9
29	1.3345	1.7758	2.3566	3.1187	4.1161	5.4184	7.1143	9.3173	12.172	15.863	26.750	44.693	57.575	74.009	121.50	197.81	511.95	1285.6	3137.9	7458.1
30	1.3478	1.8114	2.4273	3.2434	4.3219	5.7435	7.6123	10.063	13.268	17.449	29.960	50.950	66.212	85.850	143.37	237.38	634.82	1645.5	4142.1	10143
40	1.4889	2.2080	3.2620	4.8010	7.0400	10.286	14.974	21.725	31.409	45.259	93.051	188.88	267.86	378.72	750.38	1469.8	5455.9	19427	66521	
50	1.6446	2.6916	4.3839	7.1067	11.467	18.420	29.457	46.902	74.358	117.39	289.00	700.23	1083.7	1670.7	3927.4	9100.4	46890			
60	1.8167	3.2810	5.8916	10.520	18.679	32.988	57.946	101.26	176.03	304.48	897.60	2595.9	4384.0	7370.2	20555	56348				

CAPITAL BUDGET MANUAL/117

Table B: Amount to which $1 per period will accumulate

Number of Periods	1%	2%	3%	4%	5%	6%	7%	8%	9%	10%	12%	14%	15%	16%	18%	20%	24%	28%	32%	36%
1	1.0000	1.0000	1.0000	1.0000	1.0000	1.0000	1.0000	1.0000	1.0000	1.0000	1.0000	1.0000	1.0000	1.0000	1.0000	1.0000	1.0000	1.0000	1.0000	1.0000
2	2.0100	2.0200	2.0300	2.0400	2.0500	2.0600	2.0700	2.0800	2.0900	2.1000	2.1200	2.1400	2.1500	2.1600	2.1800	2.2000	2.2400	2.2800	2.3200	2.3600
3	3.0301	3.0604	3.0909	3.1216	3.1525	3.1836	3.2149	3.2464	3.2781	3.3100	3.3744	3.4396	3.4725	3.5056	3.5724	3.6400	3.7776	3.9184	4.0624	4.2096
4	4.0604	4.1216	4.1836	4.2465	4.3101	4.3746	4.4399	4.5061	4.5731	4.6410	4.7793	4.9211	4.9934	5.0665	5.2154	5.3680	5.6842	6.0156	6.3624	6.7251
5	5.1010	5.2040	5.3091	5.4163	5.5256	5.6371	5.7507	5.8666	5.9847	6.1051	6.3528	6.6101	6.7424	6.8771	7.1542	7.4416	8.0484	8.6999	9.3983	10.146
6	6.1520	6.3081	6.4684	6.6330	6.8019	6.9753	7.1533	7.3359	7.5233	7.7156	8.1152	8.5355	8.7537	8.9775	9.4420	9.9299	10.980	12.136	13.406	14.799
7	7.2135	7.4343	7.6625	7.8983	8.1420	8.3938	8.6540	8.9228	9.2004	9.4872	10.089	10.730	11.067	11.414	12.142	12.916	14.615	16.534	18.696	21.126
8	8.2857	8.5830	8.8923	9.2142	9.5491	9.8975	10.260	10.637	11.028	11.436	12.300	13.233	13.727	14.240	15.327	16.499	19.123	22.163	25.678	29.732
9	9.3685	9.7546	10.159	10.583	11.027	11.491	11.978	12.488	13.021	13.579	14.776	16.085	16.786	17.519	19.086	20.799	24.712	29.369	34.895	41.435
10	10.462	10.950	11.464	12.006	12.578	13.181	13.816	14.487	15.193	15.937	17.549	19.337	20.304	21.321	23.521	25.959	31.643	38.593	47.062	57.352
11	11.567	12.169	12.808	13.486	14.207	14.972	15.784	16.645	17.560	18.531	20.655	23.045	24.349	25.733	28.755	32.150	40.238	50.398	63.122	78.998
12	12.683	13.412	14.192	15.026	15.917	16.870	17.888	18.977	20.141	21.384	24.133	27.271	29.002	30.850	34.931	39.581	50.895	65.510	84.320	108.44
13	13.809	14.680	15.618	16.627	17.713	18.882	20.141	21.495	22.953	24.523	28.029	32.089	34.352	36.786	42.219	48.497	64.110	84.853	112.30	148.47
14	14.947	15.974	17.086	18.292	19.599	21.015	22.550	24.215	26.019	27.975	32.393	37.581	40.505	43.672	50.818	59.196	80.496	109.61	149.24	202.93
15	16.097	17.293	18.599	20.024	21.579	23.276	25.129	27.152	29.361	31.772	37.280	43.842	47.580	51.660	60.965	72.035	100.82	141.30	198.00	276.98
16	17.258	18.639	20.157	21.825	23.657	25.673	27.888	30.324	33.003	35.950	42.753	50.980	55.717	60.925	72.939	87.442	126.01	181.87	262.36	377.69
17	18.430	20.012	21.762	23.698	25.840	28.213	30.840	33.750	36.974	40.545	48.884	59.118	65.075	71.673	87.068	105.93	157.25	233.79	347.31	514.66
18	19.615	21.412	23.414	25.645	28.132	30.906	33.999	37.450	41.301	45.599	55.750	68.394	75.836	84.141	103.74	128.12	195.99	300.25	459.45	700.94
19	20.811	22.841	25.117	27.671	30.539	33.760	37.379	41.446	46.018	51.159	63.440	78.969	88.212	98.603	123.41	154.74	244.03	385.32	607.47	954.28
20	22.019	24.297	26.870	29.778	33.066	36.786	40.995	45.762	51.160	57.275	72.052	91.025	102.44	115.38	146.63	186.69	303.60	494.21	802.86	1298.8
21	23.239	25.783	28.676	31.969	35.719	39.992	44.865	50.423	56.765	64.002	81.699	104.77	118.81	134.84	174.02	225.03	377.46	633.59	1060.8	1767.4
22	24.472	27.299	30.537	34.248	38.505	43.392	49.006	55.457	62.873	71.403	92.503	120.44	137.63	157.41	206.34	271.03	469.06	812.00	1401.2	2404.7
23	25.716	28.845	32.453	36.618	41.430	46.996	53.436	60.893	69.532	79.543	104.60	138.30	159.28	183.60	244.49	326.24	582.63	1040.4	1850.6	3271.3
24	26.973	30.422	34.426	39.083	44.502	50.816	58.177	66.765	76.790	88.497	118.16	158.66	184.17	213.98	289.49	392.48	723.46	1332.7	2443.8	4450.0
25	28.243	32.030	36.459	41.646	47.727	54.865	63.249	73.106	84.701	98.347	133.33	181.87	212.79	249.21	342.60	471.98	898.09	1706.8	3226.8	6053.0
26	29.526	33.671	38.553	44.312	51.113	59.156	68.676	79.954	93.324	109.18	150.33	208.33	245.71	290.09	405.27	567.38	1114.6	2185.7	4260.4	8233.1
27	30.821	35.344	40.710	47.084	54.669	63.706	74.484	87.351	102.72	121.10	169.37	238.50	283.57	337.50	479.22	681.85	1383.1	2798.7	5624.8	11198.0
28	32.129	37.051	42.931	49.968	56.403	68.528	80.698	95.339	112.97	134.21	190.70	272.89	327.10	392.50	566.48	819.22	1716.1	3583.3	7425.7	15230.3
29	33.450	38.792	45.219	52.966	62.323	73.640	87.347	103.97	124.14	148.63	214.58	312.09	377.17	456.30	669.45	984.07	2129.0	4587.7	9802.9	20714.2
30	34.785	40.568	47.575	56.085	66.439	79.058	94.461	113.28	136.31	164.49	241.33	356.79	434.75	530.31	790.95	1181.9	2640.9	5873.2	12941.	28172.3
40	48.886	60.402	75.401	95.026	120.80	154.76	199.64	259.06	337.88	442.59	767.09	1342.0	1779.1	2360.8	4163.2	7343.9	22729.	69377.		
50	64.463	84.579	112.80	152.67	209.35	290.34	406.53	573.77	815.08	1163.9	2400.0	4994.5	7217.7	10436.	21813.	45497.				
60	81.670	114.05	163.05	237.99	353.58	533.13	813.52	1253.2	1944.8	3034.8	7471.6	18535.	29220.	46058.						

118/CAPITAL BUDGETING FOR CITY AND COUNTY GOVERNMENTS

Table C: Present value of $1

Period	1%	2%	3%	4%	5%	6%	7%	8%	9%	10%	12%	14%	15%	16%	18%	20%	24%	28%	32%	36%
1	.9901	.9804	.9709	.9615	.9524	.9434	.9346	.9259	.9174	.9091	.8929	.8772	.8696	.8621	.8475	.8333	.8065	.7813	.7576	.7353
2	.9803	.9612	.9426	.9246	.9070	.8900	.8734	.8573	.8417	.8264	.7972	.7695	.7561	.7432	.7182	.6944	.6504	.6104	.5739	.5407
3	.9706	.9423	.9151	.8890	.8638	.8396	.8163	.7938	.7722	.7513	.7118	.6750	.6575	.6407	.6086	.5787	.5245	.4768	.4348	.3975
4	.9610	.9238	.8885	.8548	.8227	.7921	.7629	.7350	.7084	.6830	.6355	.5921	.5718	.5523	.5158	.4823	.4230	.3725	.3294	.2923
5	.9515	.9057	.8626	.8219	.7835	.7473	.7130	.6806	.6499	.6209	.5674	.5194	.4972	.4761	.4371	.4019	.3411	.2910	.2495	.2149
6	.9420	.8880	.8375	.7903	.7462	.7050	.6663	.6302	.5963	.5645	.5066	.4556	.4323	.4104	.3704	.3349	.2751	.2274	.1890	.1580
7	.9327	.8706	.8131	.7599	.7107	.6651	.6227	.5835	.5470	.5132	.4523	.3996	.3759	.3538	.3139	.2791	.2218	.1776	.1432	.1162
8	.9235	.8535	.7894	.7307	.6768	.6274	.5820	.5403	.5019	.4665	.4039	.3506	.3269	.3050	.2660	.2326	.1789	.1388	.1085	.0854
9	.9143	.8368	.7664	.7026	.6446	.5919	.5439	.5002	.4604	.4241	.3606	.3075	.2843	.2630	.2255	.1938	.1443	.1084	.0822	.0628
10	.9053	.8203	.7441	.6756	.6139	.5584	.5083	.4632	.4224	.3855	.3220	.2697	.2472	.2267	.1911	.1615	.1164	.0847	.0623	.0462
11	.8963	.8043	.7224	.6496	.5847	.5268	.4751	.4289	.3875	.3505	.2875	.2366	.2149	.1954	.1619	.1346	.0938	.0662	.0472	.0340
12	.8874	.7885	.7014	.6246	.5568	.4970	.4440	.3971	.3555	.3186	.2567	.2076	.1869	.1685	.1372	.1122	.0757	.0517	.0357	.0250
13	.8787	.7730	.6810	.6006	.5303	.4688	.4150	.3677	.3262	.2897	.2292	.1821	.1625	.1452	.1163	.0935	.0610	.0404	.0271	.0184
14	.8700	.7579	.6611	.5775	.5051	.4423	.3878	.3405	.2992	.2633	.2046	.1597	.1413	.1252	.0985	.0779	.0492	.0316	.0205	.0135
15	.8613	.7430	.6419	.5553	.4810	.4173	.3624	.3152	.2745	.2394	.1827	.1401	.1229	.1079	.0835	.0649	.0397	.0247	.0155	.0099
16	.8528	.7284	.6232	.5339	.4581	.3936	.3387	.2919	.2519	.2176	.1631	.1229	.1069	.0930	.0708	.0541	.0320	.0193	.0118	.0073
17	.8444	.7142	.6050	.5134	.4363	.3714	.3166	.2703	.2311	.1978	.1456	.1078	.0929	.0802	.0600	.0451	.0258	.0150	.0089	.0054
18	.8360	.7002	.5874	.4936	.4155	.3503	.2959	.2502	.2120	.1799	.1300	.0946	.0808	.0691	.0508	.0376	.0208	.0118	.0068	.0039
19	.8277	.6864	.5703	.4746	.3957	.3305	.2765	.2317	.1945	.1635	.1161	.0829	.0703	.0596	.0431	.0313	.0168	.0092	.0051	.0029
20	.8195	.6730	.5537	.4564	.3769	.3118	.2584	.2145	.1784	.1486	.1037	.0728	.0611	.0514	.0365	.0261	.0135	.0072	.0039	.0021
21	.8114	.6598	.5375	.4388	.3589	.2942	.2415	.1987	.1637	.1351	.0926	.0638	.0531	.0443	.0309	.0217	.0109	.0056	.0029	.0016
22	.8034	.6468	.5219	.4220	.3418	.2775	.2257	.1839	.1502	.1228	.0826	.0560	.0462	.0382	.0262	.0181	.0088	.0044	.0022	.0012
23	.7954	.6342	.5067	.4057	.3256	.2618	.2109	.1703	.1378	.1117	.0738	.0491	.0402	.0329	.0222	.0151	.0071	.0034	.0017	.0008
24	.7876	.6217	.4919	.3901	.3101	.2470	.1971	.1577	.1264	.1015	.0659	.0431	.0349	.0284	.0188	.0126	.0057	.0027	.0013	.0006
25	.7798	.6095	.4776	.3751	.2953	.2330	.1842	.1460	.1160	.0923	.0588	.0378	.0304	.0245	.0160	.0105	.0046	.0021	.0010	.0005
26	.7720	.5976	.4637	.3607	.2812	.2198	.1722	.1352	.1064	.0839	.0525	.0331	.0264	.0211	.0135	.0087	.0037	.0016	.0007	.0003
27	.7644	.5859	.4502	.3468	.2678	.2074	.1609	.1252	.0976	.0763	.0469	.0291	.0230	.0182	.0115	.0073	.0030	.0013	.0006	.0002
28	.7568	.5744	.4371	.3335	.2551	.1956	.1504	.1159	.0895	.0693	.0419	.0255	.0200	.0157	.0097	.0061	.0024	.0010	.0004	.0002
29	.7493	.5631	.4243	.3207	.2429	.1846	.1406	.1073	.0822	.0630	.0374	.0224	.0174	.0135	.0082	.0051	.0020	.0008	.0003	.0002
30	.7419	.5521	.4120	.3083	.2314	.1741	.1314	.0994	.0754	.0573	.0334	.0196	.0151	.0116	.0070	.0042	.0016	.0006	.0002	.0001
35	.7059	.5000	.3554	.2534	.1813	.1301	.0937	.0676	.0490	.0356	.0189	.0102	.0075	.0055	.0030	.0017	.0005	.0002	.0001	.0001
40	.6717	.4529	.3066	.2083	.1420	.0972	.0668	.0460	.0318	.0221	.0107	.0053	.0037	.0026	.0013	.0007	.0002	.0001		
45	.6391	.4102	.2644	.1712	.1113	.0727	.0476	.0313	.0207	.0137	.0061	.0027	.0019	.0013	.0006	.0003	.0001			
50	.6080	.3715	.2281	.1407	.0872	.0543	.0339	.0213	.0134	.0085	.0035	.0014	.0009	.0006	.0003	.0001				
55	.5785	.3365	.1968	.1157	.0683	.0406	.0242	.0145	.0087	.0053	.0020	.0007	.0005	.0003	.0001					

CHAPTER

A COMPUTER-ASSISTED VERSION OF THE PLANNING MODEL

The purpose of this chapter is to describe the design and operation of a computer-assisted version of the Capital Budget Planning Model and illustrate its application. The version of the model presented here operates on IBM PC/XT and compatible microcomputers. It is an application that runs on the well-known Lotus 1-2-3™ spreadsheet software.[1] While many readers may easily adapt the methodology presented in the preceding chapters to any one of the many available microcomputer spreadsheet software packages, a Lotus 1-2-3 template is available containing an easy-to-use, interactive version of the Capital Budget Planning Model.

While the hand-operated, or accounting-based, technique presented in Chapter 5 will provide entirely satisfactory analyses of planned capital expenditures, the computer-assisted version will perform the tasks quicker and with greater accuracy and reliability. The speed (and hence, the convenience) with which the computer is able to handle the necessary calculations is especially important when circumstances indicate a need to perform sensitivity analyses on a number of planning variables or when a municipality's capital budget contains a number of projects to be analyzed.

To use the template version of the model, the user must have access to an IBM PC/XT (or compatible) with 512K of memory, Lotus 1-2-3™ version 1A or version 2 software, and DOS 2.1 or later. Those who do not have this type of system available need not feel that their capital budgeting systems are in any way inferior to others, insofar as the *quality* of the system is concerned. Both the hand-operated and computer-assisted versions of the model will produce identical results from a given set of input data.

The Clayton City Park example will be used again, this time to illustrate the computer-assisted version of the model. The discussion begins by presenting the format in which the computer program accepts the financial planning estimates. Next, the output for each of the four financing options—gifts and grants, property tax increase, revenue bonds, and general obligation bonds—is presented. Finally, sensitivity analysis is performed on several controllable planning estimates in order to illustrate how the model can best be employed in the capital budgeting process.

Input Format

The template on which the computer-assisted version of the model runs has been prepared in the *interactive mode*; that is, the program provides instructions or asks questions that serve as guides to both data input and output selection. The input formats are presented in Exhibits 6-1 through 6-6 exactly as they appear on the computer screen. Notice that

(*Text continued on page* 127)

Exhibit 6-1: **First Data Entry Screen**

```
F8: 1788                                                          READY

      A         B         C         D         E         F
 1  ═══════════════════════════════════════════════════════════════════
 2       17-Oct-86     DATA ENTRY SCREEN     Revision:     4
 3  ═══════════════════════════════════════════════════════════════════
 4
 5  PROJECT TITLE:   CLAYTON CITY PARK
 6
 7
 8  A.  What year is the project scheduled to begin ?----    1988
 9      What is the current year ?--------------------------    1987
10      Enter the year in which the project is scheduled
11      to be completed ------------------------------------    1997
12
13  B.  Capital Costs
14      1. a.  Contract price of construction--------------  $866,670
15         b.  Cost of approved changes-------------------        $0
16         c.  Engineering and contingency costs----------  $133,330
17         d.     Total Capital Costs---------------------$1,000,000
18
19
20                                                              CAPS
```

Exhibit 6-2: **Second Data Entry Screen**

B29: (C0) 250000   READY

```
           A       B           C           D           E           F

 1
 2              17-Oct-86   DATA ENTRY SCREEN       Revision:      4
 3
22         C. Capital Costs and       D. Operating Costs and Revenues
23            Equipment Purchases:       Covering the Life of the Project:
24
25                                    Operating,    Surplus    Operating and
26              Capital    Equipment  Maintenance   From       Non-operating
27     Year     Costs      Purchases  Costs         Operations Revenues
28     ----     -------    ---------  -----------   ---------- -------------
29     1988     $250,000   $0         $0            $0         $0
30     1989     $350,000   $0         $0            $0         $0
31     1990     $400,000   $150,000   $0            $0         $0
32     1991     $0         $0         $60,000       $0         $71,000
33     1992     $0         $0         $60,000       $0         $71,000
34     1993     $0         $0         $60,000       $0         $71,000
35     1994     $0         $0         $60,000       $0         $71,000
36     1995     $0         $0         $60,000       $0         $71,000
37     1996     $0         $0         $60,000       $0         $71,000
38     1997     $0         $0         $60,000       $0         $71,000
```

CALC

Exhibit 6-3: **Third Data Entry Screen**

```
17:                                                              READY

        I         J          K          L          M         N
═══════════════════════════════════════════════════════════════════════
 1
 2            17-Oct-86    DATA ENTRY SCREEN    Revision:    4
 3  ═══════════════════════════════════════════════════════════════════
 4  PROJECT TITLE:   CLAYTON CITY PARK
 5    E.  Inflation Rates
 6        1.  Schedule of inflation rates (round to nearest one percent
 7            and enter as a decimal):
 8                      Category                    Annual Inflation Rate
 9                      --------                    ---------------------
10            a.  Construction----------------------------        18.00%
11            b.  Equipment-------------------------------         8.00%
12            c.  Operation/Maintenance-------------------         7.00%
13            d.  Revenues (maximum)----------------------         4.50%
14
15    F.  Cash Management
16        1.  Size of current unencumbered, nondesignated cash surplus
17            available to cover temporary cash deficits for the
18            project:           $0
19
20
                                                      CALC      CAPS
```

Exhibit 6-4: **Fourth Data Entry Screen**

```
N24: (P2) 0.09                                                      READY
================================================================================
       I          J           K           L           M           N
================================================================================
              17-Oct-86      DATA ENTRY SCREEN      Revision:
================================================================================

       2.  Expected average rate of return from the investment of
           cash surplus over the life of the project to the
           nearest one percent (enter as a decimal):           9.00%

    6. Municipal Tax Assessment
       1.  Total property tax assessment----------------  $33,000,000
       2.  Expected average annual growth rate of
           the tax assessment to the nearest one
           percent (enter as a decimal)-----------------         2.00%
       3.  Maximum tax increase in mills the governing
           body will enact in support of the project's
           operations-----------------------------------             2
       4.  Year in which tax increase will be
           enacted--------------------------------------          1988

                                                                  CALC
```

Exhibit 6-5: **Fifth Data Entry Screen**

```
N42: 1                                                              READY

         I         J          K            L          M           N
======================================================================
 1                17-Oct-86      DATA ENTRY SCREEN      Revision:    4
 2  ==================================================================
 3
39       H.   Gifts and Grants
40            1.  Will any portion of the project be financed with funds
41                other than those supplied by loans or the sale of
42                bonds ? (Enter 1 for YES, 0 for NO)                1
43
44            Surplus                                             Percent
45    Year     Cash      Grants       Other        Total          Of Total
46    ----    -------   ---------   ---------    ---------        --------
47    1988      $0      $300,000     $80,000     $380,000          63.3%
48    1989      $0       $50,000     $60,000     $110,000          18.3%
49    1990      $0       $50,000     $40,000      $90,000          15.0%
50    1991      $0           $0     $20,000      $20,000           3.3%
51    1992      $0           $0          $0           $0           0.0%
52    1993      $0           $0          $0           $0           0.0%
53    1994      $0           $0          $0           $0           0.0%
54    1995      $0           $0          $0           $0           0.0%
55    1996      $0           $0          $0           $0           0.0%
                                                      CALC
```

Exhibit 6-6: Sixth Data Entry Screen

```
U7: (F2) 0.07                                                    READY

     O         P         Q         R         S         T         U
============================================================================
1
2        17-Oct-86         DATA ENTRY SCREEN      Revision:     4
3   ========================================================================
4   PROJECT TITLE:   CLAYTON CITY PARK
5    1.  Debt Financing
6        1. At what rate of interest can long-term funds
7           be acquired (Enter as a decimal)--------------------    7.00%
8        2. Will the debt be repaid with: (Enter 1 for YES, 0 for NO)
9           a. Operating revenues-----------------------------         1
10          b. Tax revenues-----------------------------------         1
11       3. What is the maximum amount of debt the municipality
12          can currently raise------------------------------ $5,000,000
13       4. What year will the bond issue be completely
14          retired-------------------------------------------     1997
15       5. What year will the first sinking fund payment
16          (loan payment) be due-----------------------------     1988
17       6. What year will the proceeds of the bond issue
18          be available-------------------------------------      1987
19       7. Short-term borrowing rate (Enter as decimal)------     7.5%
20
                                                      CALC    CAPS
```

(*Text continued from page* 120)

these data entry screens bear a close resemblance to the Program Description Form contained in the capital budgeting manual presented in Chapter 5. Hence, the information may be recorded first on a copy of that form and then transferred to the computer during the data entry process.

Once the planning parameters have been established and the data prepared for entry into the planning model, the Lotus 1-2-3 software should be loaded into the computer according to the instructions provided in the software documentation. When Lotus indicates it is in the ready mode, the disk containing the capital budgeting template should be inserted into drive B in the computer or copied onto the hard disk (if the computer is thus equipped) in the appropriate directory from where it may subsequently be called into the Lotus spreadsheet. The template is then called up to the screen by typing /*File Retrieve* and then the file name, CAPITAL, followed by a return ↵.

After the model appears on the screen, the interactive mode of the template is initiated. At this point the cursor will move to the first data entry point, shown as cell C5 in Exhibit 6-1, where the project title is to be entered. After the title, CLAYTON CITY PARK, is typed, it is entered by striking the return key ↵, at which time the cursor will jump to cell F8. Since the Clayton City Park project will begin in 1987, that figure is typed in and entered by striking the return key. The cursor will jump to the next cell (F9, in this case) and continue moving forward as the data are entered.

Data errors may be corrected in the interactive mode by using the directional arrows on the cursor pad to move the cursor to the cell containing the error. After an error has been corrected, use the cursor pad to either move to another error or return the cursor to the data entry point from which it was first removed. If you strike the return key rather than use the cursor pad to return the cursor to the last data entry point, the new data will be entered into the model, but the cursor will jump to the next data entry point in the original sequence.

Data entry should be accomplished in accordance with the instructions contained in the Program Description Form in Chapter 5. When all the data have been entered, the program will ask whether you would like to have the input form printed for verification (see Exhibit 6-7). In most cases, having the printed form for reference is a good idea. Not only does it provide a useful and convenient guide for verifying the input data, but it also serves as a handy reference for conducting sensitivity analysis, as will be illustrated later.

By striking 1 and return, you will cause the input form to be printed, and by striking 0, you will cause the computer to move on to the next screen, shown in Exhibit 6-8. By entering 1, 2, or 3, respectively, into this screen, you will start processing the data, begin the input cycle again to make changes in the data, or exit from the program.

Computer Output

The computer-assisted version of the planning model, like the accounting-based version, will enable the analyst to examine four financing options: (1) gifts and pledges, (2) property tax increases, (3) revenue bonds, and (4) general obligation bonds. For each option, the model will determine whether or not the project is viable, and if it is not, it will calculate the financial requirements necessary to achieve project viability.

The model will also construct a "Chart of Cash Flows" for each option, detailing annual cash inflows, cash outflows, and project cash balances over the life of the project. In those instances in which the project is not financially viable, the chart of cash flows will show its year-end cash balances in both its nonviable and viable states. That is, it will create both a *nonviable* financing package that stays within the constraints imposed by the input data and a *viable* financing

Exhibit 6-7: **Seventh Data Entry Screen**

```
EU11:                                                                    READY
    EF      EU      ER      EQ      ET      EU      EV      EW

                   PRINT INPUT FORM FOR VERIFICATION ?

                            ENTER 1 FOR YES            0

                            ENTER 0 FOR NO


 1
 2
 3
 4
 5
 6
 7
 8
 9
10
11
12
13
14
15
16
17
18
19
20
                                                          CALC      CAPS
```

Exhibit 6-8: **Eighth Data Entry Screen**

```
EU32: 2                                                              READY

      EF       EG       EA       ES       ET       EU       EV       EW


              1. INPUT DATA CORRECT, EXECUTE PROGRAM

              2. RETURN TO INPUT

              3. EXIT PROGRAM

              Enter Selection............ 2


                                                                CALC  CAPS
```

package that ignores those constraints. Printing the charts is optional.

The data contained in Exhibits 6-1 through 6-6 were used to generate financial solutions under the four options for the Clayton City Park project. Some changes have been made to the planning estimates used in Chapter 5 in order to better illustrate the computer-assisted version of the model.

The time required for the computer to calculate the solutions to the planning model will depend on the number of years in the planning period and the clock speed of the computer on which the model is run. The Clayton City Park project, when run on a PC/XT compatible computer operating at a low speed, required five and one-half minutes to generate a set of solutions. An AT compatible computer will perform the task in about three and one-half minutes.

Once the calculations have been completed, the model will generate a printing menu on the screen. This menu is illustrated in Exhibit 6-9. By selecting menu item 1, the user can look at the basic solutions to, and cash-flow tables for, all four funding options. Selecting item 2 will generate the solutions only, and item 3 will print the cash-flow tables only. The user can look at the supporting calculations, from which all of the solutions are derived, by selecting menu item 4.

Menu item 5 is included as a convenience for the user in those instances in which the model is being run a number of times under differing assumptions regarding the project's planning parameters. Once the results of the current run have been printed, the solution can be erased from the worksheet, and the user can return to the data entry screens to make changes in the planning parameters and rerun the model. Note that the calculations must be erased before a new set of solutions is attempted. Otherwise, the model will not work properly.

Finally, by selecting item 6, the user can exit the program. The model will provide the user with the opportunity to save

Exhibit 6-9: Printing Menu

```
ET58: 6                                                         READY
   EP     EQ     ER     ES     ET     EU     EV     EW
43
44
45
46        1. PRINT ALL SCHEDULES (6 THROUGH 12D)
47
48        2. PRINT SCHEDULES 6 THROUGH 9 ONLY
49
50        3. PRINT SCHEDULES 12A THROUGH 12D ONLY
51
52        4. PRINT SUPPORTING CALCULATIONS (1 THROUGH 5)
53
54        5. ERASE ALL CALCULATIONS AND RETURN TO INPUT
55
56        6. EXIT PROGRAM
57
58        Enter Selection.............  6                      CALC
59
```

the input data and the calculations if item 6 is selected. The model will ask the user to name the file if the worksheet is to be saved.

The solutions to the Clayton City Park project are presented and discussed in the following sections.

Gifts and Grants

The printed output contains three schedules that are relevant to the gifts and grants option. These are presented in Exhibits 6-10 through 6-12. Schedule 6 (Exhibit 6-10) calculates the nominal dollar amount of funding required to fully finance the project out of donated funds only. Line 3 in the schedule shows the nominal fund-raising goal, assuming that the timing of the cash receipts from the fund-raising campaign is as presented in the data input section. Line 4 lists the total amount of gifts anticipated in the financial plan, and the last line in the schedule lists the

(*Text continued on page* 136)

Exhibit 6-10: **Schedule 6, Gifts and Grants Option**

```
===============================================================================
                              SCHEDULE 6
                        GIFTS AND GRANTS OPTION
-------------------------------------------------------------------------------
               Calculation of Nominal Dollar Amount for Funding
               --------------------------------------------------

    1. Present value of net project costs------------------    $872,022

    2. Present value factor-------------------------------     0.87479

    3. Line 1 divided by Line 2---------------------------     $996,837

    4. Total expected gifts and grants--------------------     $600,000

       The project will produce a surplus (deficit) of:       ($396,837)
```

Exhibit 6-11: **Schedule 12A, Actual Project Cash Flows Under Gifts and Grants Option**

SCHEDULE 12A ACTUAL PROJECT CASH FLOWS UNDER GIFTS AND GRANTS OPTION

Year	Total Inflated Costs	Operating Revenues	Actual Gifts And Grants	Net Cash Flow	Beginning Cash Balance	Interest Earned(Paid)	Ending Cash Balance
Current: 1987							
Project:							
1988	$250,000	$0	$380,000	$130,000	$0	$0	$130,000
1989	$350,000	$0	$110,000	($240,000)	$130,000	$11,700	($98,300)
1990	$588,957	$0	$90,000	($498,957)	($98,300)	($8,847)	($606,104)
1991	$78,648	$108,519	$20,000	$49,871	($606,104)	($54,549)	($610,782)
1992	$84,153	$113,403	$0	$29,249	($610,782)	($54,970)	($636,503)
1993	$90,044	$118,506	$0	$28,462	($636,503)	($57,285)	($665,326)
1994	$96,347	$123,838	$0	$27,492	($665,326)	($59,879)	($697,714)
1995	$103,091	$129,411	$0	$26,320	($697,714)	($62,794)	($734,188)
1996	$110,308	$135,235	$0	$24,927	($734,188)	($66,077)	($775,338)
1997	$118,029	$141,320	$0	$23,291	($775,338)	($69,780)	($821,827)

The project will produce a surplus (deficit) of: ($396,837)

Exhibit 6-12: **Schedule 12A, Required Project Cash Flows Under Gifts and Grants Option**

SCHEDULE 12A REQUIRED PROJECT CASH FLOWS UNDER GIFTS AND GRANTS OPTION

Year	Total Inflated Costs	Operating Revenues	Required Gifts And Grants	Net Cash Flow	Beginning Cash Balance	Interest Earned(Paid)	Ending Cash Balance
Current:							
1987							
Project:							
1988	$250,000	$0	$631,330	$381,330	$0	$0	$381,330
1989	$350,000	$0	$182,753	($167,247)	$381,330	$34,320	$248,403
1990	$588,957	$0	$149,526	($439,431)	$248,403	$22,356	($168,672)
1991	$78,648	$108,519	$33,228	$63,099	($168,672)	($15,180)	($120,753)
1992	$84,153	$113,403	$0	$29,249	($120,753)	($10,868)	($102,371)
1993	$90,044	$118,506	$0	$28,462	($102,371)	($9,213)	($83,123)
1994	$96,347	$123,838	$0	$27,492	($83,123)	($7,481)	($63,112)
1995	$103,091	$129,411	$0	$26,320	($63,112)	($5,680)	($42,473)
1996	$110,308	$135,235	$0	$24,927	($42,473)	($3,823)	($21,368)
1997	$118,029	$141,320	$0	$23,291	($21,368)	($1,923)	$0

Because the short-term borrowing rate is higher than the rate of return from the investment of cash surplus, the project will incur an added interest cost of................................. $5,963.

(Text continued from page 133)

project's overall surplus or deficit. In this example, the Clayton City Park project requires $396,837 more in donated funds to achieve financial viability.

Exhibit 6-11 and Exhibit 6-12, both designated as Schedule 12A, show the *actual* and *required* project cash flows, respectively, under the gifts and grants option. The actual cash-flow table (Exhibit 6-11) shows the project's annual cash flow under the assumption, in this example, that the level of donated funds will reach the planned amount of $600,000. As is clear from the far right column, the project's year-end cash balances become negative in 1989, and the annual cash deficit continues to grow throughout the planning period.

Exhibit 6-12 shows what would happen if the city raised an additional $396,837 of donated funds and allocated it to the city park project. In this case the operating revenues would repay by the final year the deficit cash position incurred early in the project. Additionally, the cash-flow table shows that if the city chose to borrow to cover the negative cash position, an incremental interest cost of $5,963 would have to be covered from some source or another. This incremental interest cost arises because the short-term borrowing rate is one-half of one percent greater than the rate of return the city realizes on its investment of surplus funds.

Tax Increase Option

Schedule 7 shown in Exhibit 6-13 calculates the funding requirements under the tax increase option. The model assumes that the city will raise the $600,000 in donated funds and make up the difference, if any, with a tax increase of up to 2 mills. Schedule 7 indicates that the 2-mill tax increase will produce a project surplus of $110,216 and that a 1.518 mill increase is all that will be needed to achieve financial viability for the Clayton City Park project.

The actual and required cash-flow tables (Schedules 12B) are presented in Exhibits 6-14 and 6-15, respectively. Note

Exhibit 6-13: **Schedule 7, Tax Increase Option**

```
===================================================================
                            SCHEDULE 7
                        TAX INCREASE OPTION
===================================================================
                  Calculation of Funding Requirements
                  ----------------------------------

    1. Present value of inflation-adjusted net costs----    $872,022

    2. Present value of tax revenues at    2 mills-------   $457,365

    3. Line 1 minus Line 2-------------------------------   $414,658

    4. Present value of gifts and grants----------------    $524,874


        The project will produce a surplus (deficit) of:    $110,216
        The approximate millage rate change is:                1.5180
```

that the third and fourth columns of Exhibit 6-15 contain the tax revenues from a 2-mill and a 1.518-mill tax increase, respectively, so that the planned and required tax revenues can be compared more readily. Note also that the cash flows from the tax increase option will require the project to incur an additional short-term interest cost of $18,034 over the planning period.

Revenue Bond Option

In order to issue revenue bonds for a particular project, the project must generate revenues, of course. Furthermore, the revenues must be sufficiently large to amortize the bond issue over the planning period. Schedule 8 (Exhibit 6-16) presents the results of the model's calculations of the

(Text continued on page 141)

Exhibit 6-14: **Schedule 12B, Actual Project Cash Flows Under Tax Increase Option**

SCHEDULE 12B ACTUAL PROJECT CASH FLOWS UNDER TAX INCREASE OPTION

Year	Total Inflated Costs	Tax Revenues	Gifts, Grants Operating Revenues	Net Cash Flow	Beginning Cash Balance	Interest Earned(Paid)	Ending Cash Balance
Current:							
1987							
Project:							
1988	$250,000	$66,000	$380,000	$196,000	$0	$0	$196,000
1989	$350,000	$67,320	$110,000	($172,680)	$196,000	$17,640	$40,960
1990	$588,957	$68,666	$90,000	($430,290)	$40,960	$3,686	($385,644)
1991	$78,648	$70,040	$128,519	$119,911	($385,644)	($34,708)	($300,441)
1992	$84,153	$71,441	$113,403	$100,690	($300,441)	($27,040)	($226,790)
1993	$90,044	$72,869	$118,506	$101,331	($226,790)	($20,411)	($145,870)
1994	$96,347	$74,327	$123,838	$101,818	($145,870)	($13,128)	($57,181)
1995	$103,091	$75,813	$129,411	$102,133	($57,181)	($5,146)	$39,806
1996	$110,308	$77,330	$135,235	$102,257	$39,806	$3,583	$145,646
1997	$118,029	$78,876	$141,320	$102,167	$145,646	$13,108	$260,921

The project will produce a surplus (deficit) of: $110,216
The approximate millage rate change is........ 1.5180

Exhibit 6-15: **Schedule 12B, Required Project Cash Flows Under Tax Increase Option**

SCHEDULE 12B REQUIRED PROJECT CASH FLOWS UNDER TAX INCREASE OPTION

Year	Total Inflated Costs	Tax Revenues	Required Tax Revenues	Net Cash Flow	Beginning Cash Balance	Interest Earned(Paid)	Ending Cash Balance
Current:							
1987							
Project:							
1988	$250,000	$66,000	$50,095	$180,095	$0	$0	$180,095
1989	$350,000	$67,320	$51,097	($188,903)	$180,095	$16,209	$7,401
1990	$588,957	$68,656	$52,119	($446,838)	$7,401	$666	($438,770)
1991	$78,648	$70,040	$53,162	$103,033	($438,770)	($39,489)	($375,227)
1992	$84,153	$71,441	$54,225	$83,474	($375,227)	($33,770)	($325,523)
1993	$90,044	$72,859	$55,309	$83,771	($325,523)	($29,297)	($271,049)
1994	$96,347	$74,327	$56,415	$83,907	($271,049)	($24,344)	($211,536)
1995	$103,091	$75,813	$57,544	$83,864	($211,536)	($19,038)	($146,711)
1996	$110,308	$77,330	$58,695	$83,622	($146,711)	($13,204)	($76,293)
1997	$118,029	$78,876	$59,869	$83,160	($76,293)	($6,866)	$0

Because the short-term borrowing rate is higher
than the rate of return from the investment of
cash surplus, the project will incur an added
interest cost of................................ $18,034

140/CAPITAL BUDGETING FOR CITY AND COUNTY GOVERNMENTS

Exhibit 6-16: **Schedule 8, Calculation of Revenue Bond Issue**

SCHEDULE 8
CALCULATION OF REVENUE BOND ISSUE

Year	NCF (e)-(d)	PV NCF @ 9.00%	PV NCF @ 7.00%	PV I @ 9.00%			
					PV I	$978,729	Maximum Bond
					PV NR	$106,706	
					PV G&b	$524,874	$120,446
Current:							
1987					Total	($347,149)	Bond Payment
Project:							$17,149
1988	$0	$0	$0	$229,358		$15,733	
1989	$0	$0	$0	$294,588		$14,434	Cash Inflow
1990	$0	$0	$0	$454,783		$13,242	
1991	$29,871	$21,162	$22,789	$0		$12,149	($3,349)
1992	$29,249	$19,010	$20,854	$0		$11,146	
1993	$28,462	$16,971	$18,965	$0		$10,225	Annual Surplus
1994	$27,492	$15,039	$17,120	$0		$9,381	
1995	$26,320	$13,209	$15,318	$0		$8,606	($52,474)
1996	$24,927	$11,477	$13,559	$0		$7,896	
1997	$23,291	$9,838	$11,840	$0		$7,244	
Total	$189,612	$106,706	$120,446	$978,729		$110,055	

Project Cash Flows Cannot Support Bond Issue.

(Text continued from page 137)

maximum bond size that can be repaid out of the project's operating revenues, the annual bond payment, and the size of the cash surplus or deficit produced out of the relevant cash flows. If, as in the present example, the project cannot be made financially viable with the issuance of revenue bonds, that fact is noted at the bottom of Schedule 9.

The six columns of figures on the left side of Schedule 9 contain the discounted cash flows needed to test the project for financial viability under this funding option. The sum of the figures in the fourth column is equal to the maximum bond issue size for the particular cash flows generated by the project.

Exhibits 6-17 and 6-18 present the cash-flow tables, labeled Schedule 12C. In this example, since the cash flows cannot support a revenue bond issue of sufficient size to achieve project financial viability, the model adds the annual deficit figure of $52,474 (see Exhibit 6-16) to the Required Gifts, Grants, and Revenues column. In other words, each year's cash inflow is increased by $52,474, thereby generating sufficient cash flow to make the Clayton City Park project viable. Again, the annual year-end cash balance deficits cause the project to incur added short-term interest costs of $13,335 (Exhibit 6-18).

General Obligation Bond Option

The final funding option examined by the model is that of general obligation bonds. Schedule 9 (Exhibit 6-19) shows the results of the calculations of the maximum bond issue size needed to fully fund the project, the annual bond payment, and the required millage rate needed to retire the bond issue. For the Clayton City Park project, the city will have to borrow $347,149 and increase taxes by 1.39 mills to achieve project financial viability. The amount designated as Additional Funds in the far-right column of Exhibit 6-

(Text continued on page 147)

Exhibit 6-17: **Schedule 12C, Actual Project Cash Flows Under Revenue Bond Option**

SCHEDULE 12C

ACTUAL PROJECT CASH FLOWS UNDER REVENUE BOND OPTION

Year	Total Inflated Costs	Debt Service Charges	Actual Gifts,Grants Revenues	Net Cash Flow	Beginning Cash Balance	Interest Earned(Paid)	Ending Cash Balance
Current:							
1987							$120,446
Project:							
1988	$250,000	$17,149	$380,000	$112,851	$120,446	$10,840	$244,137
1989	$350,000	$17,149	$110,000	($257,149)	$244,137	$21,972	$8,961
1990	$588,957	$17,149	$90,000	($516,106)	$8,961	$806	($506,338)
1991	$78,648	$17,149	$128,519	$32,723	($506,338)	($45,570)	($519,186)
1992	$84,153	$17,149	$113,403	$12,101	($519,186)	($46,727)	($553,812)
1993	$90,044	$17,149	$118,506	$11,313	($553,812)	($49,843)	($592,342)
1994	$96,347	$17,149	$123,838	$10,343	($592,342)	($53,311)	($635,310)
1995	$103,091	$17,149	$129,411	$9,171	($635,310)	($57,178)	($683,317)
1996	$110,308	$17,149	$135,235	$7,778	($683,317)	($61,499)	($737,037)
1997	$118,029	$17,149	$141,320	$6,142	($737,037)	($66,333)	($797,228)

The project will produce a surplus (deficit) of: $120,446

Exhibit 6-18: **Schedule 12C, Required Cash Flows Under Revenue Bond Option**

SCHEDULE 12C — REQUIRED PROJECT CASH FLOWS UNDER REVENUE BOND OPTION

Year	Total Inflated Costs	Debt Service Charges	Required Gifts, Grants Revenues	Net Cash Flow	Beginning Cash Balance	Interest Earned (Paid)	Ending Cash Balance
Current:							
1987							
Project:							
1988	$250,000	$17,149	$432,474	$165,325			$120,446
1989	$350,000	$17,149	$162,474	($204,675)	$120,446	$10,840	$296,611
1990	$588,957	$17,149	$142,474	($463,632)	$296,611	$26,695	$118,631
1991	$78,648	$17,149	$180,993	$85,196	$118,631	$10,677	($334,324)
1992	$84,153	$17,149	$165,876	$64,574	($334,324)	($30,089)	($279,217)
1993	$90,044	$17,149	$170,979	$63,787	($279,217)	($25,130)	($239,773)
1994	$96,347	$17,149	$176,312	$62,816	($239,773)	($21,580)	($197,565)
1995	$103,091	$17,149	$181,885	$61,645	($197,565)	($17,781)	($152,530)
1996	$110,308	$17,149	$187,708	$60,252	($152,530)	($13,728)	($104,613)
1997	$118,029	$17,149	$193,794	$58,616	($104,613)	($9,415)	($53,776)
					($53,776)	($4,840)	$0

Because the short-term borrowing rate is higher than the rate of return from the investment of cash surplus, the project will incur an added interest cost of.................................. $13,355 .

144/CAPITAL BUDGETING FOR CITY AND COUNTY GOVERNMENTS

Exhibit 6-19: **Schedule 9, Calculation of General Obligation Bond**

SCHEDULE 9
CALCULATION OF GENERAL OBLIGATION BOND

Year	NCF	PV NCF @ 9.00%	PV NCF @ 7.00%	PV I @ 9.00%		PV NC PV G&G	FV Tax	Maximum Bond
Current:								
1987						Total	$347,149	$347,149
Project:								Bond Payment
1988	$229,358	$210,420	$214,353	$229,358		$45,345	$30,275,229	$49,426
1989	$294,588	$247,949	$257,305	$294,588		$41,601	$28,330,949	Required Millage
1990	$454,783	$351,176	$371,238	$454,783		$38,166	$26,511,530	
1991	($21,162)	($14,991)	($16,144)	$0		$35,015	$24,808,955	1.39
1992	($19,010)	($12,355)	($13,554)	$0		$32,124	$23,215,719	
1993	($16,971)	($10,119)	($11,308)	$0		$29,471	$21,724,801	Additional Funds
1994	($15,039)	($8,227)	($9,365)	$0		$27,038	$20,329,630	
1995	($13,209)	($6,629)	($7,688)	$0		$24,805	$19,024,058	$500,547
1996	($11,477)	($5,284)	($6,243)	$0		$22,757	$17,802,329	
1997	($9,838)	($4,156)	($5,001)	$0		$20,878	$16,659,061	
Total	$872,022	$747,782	$773,592	$978,729		$317,200	$228,682,261	

| | | | | | | PV NC | $872,022 | |
| | | | | | | PV G&G | $524,874 | |

Exhibit 6-20: **Schedule 12D, Actual Project Cash Flows Under General Obligation Bond**

```
SCHEDULE 12D                      ACTUAL PROJECT CASH FLOWS UNDER GENERAL OBLIGATION BOND
```

Year	Total Inflated Costs	Debt Service Charges	Actual Cash Inflows	Net Cash Flow	Beginning Cash Balance	Interest Earned(Paid)	Ending Cash Balance
Current:							
1987							
Project:							
1988	$250,000	$49,426	$446,000	$146,574			$347,149
1989	$350,000	$49,426	$177,320	($222,106)	$347,149	$31,243	$524,966
1990	$588,957	$49,426	$158,666	($479,717)	$524,966	$47,247	$350,107
1991	$78,648	$49,426	$198,559	$70,485	$350,107	$31,510	($98,100)
1992	$84,153	$49,426	$184,843	$51,264	($98,100)	($8,829)	($36,444)
1993	$90,044	$49,426	$191,375	$51,905	($36,444)	($3,280)	$11,539
1994	$96,347	$49,426	$198,165	$52,392	$11,539	$1,039	$64,483
1995	$103,091	$49,426	$205,224	$52,707	$64,483	$5,803	$122,679
1996	$110,308	$49,426	$212,564	$52,830	$122,679	$11,041	$186,427
1997	$118,029	$49,426	$220,196	$52,741	$186,427	$16,778	$256,036
					$256,036	$23,043	$331,820

The project will produce a surplus (deficit) of: $153,398

Exhibit 6-21: **Schedule 12D, Required Cash Flows Under General Obligation Bond**

SCHEDULE 12D REQUIRED PROJECT CASH FLOWS UNDER GENERAL OBLIGATION BOND

Year	Total Inflated Costs	Debt Service Charges	Required Cash Inflows	Net Cash Flow	Beginning Cash Balance	Interest Earned(Paid)	Ending Cash Balance
Current:							
1987							$347,149
Project:							
1988	$250,000	$49,426	$425,774	$126,347	$347,149	$31,243	$504,739
1989	$350,000	$49,426	$156,689	($242,737)	$504,739	$45,427	$307,429
1990	$588,957	$49,426	$137,623	($500,760)	$307,429	$27,669	($165,663)
1991	$78,648	$49,426	$177,094	$49,021	($165,663)	($14,910)	($131,552)
1992	$84,153	$49,426	$162,949	$29,370	($131,552)	($11,840)	($114,021)
1993	$90,044	$49,426	$169,043	$29,573	($114,021)	($10,262)	($94,710)
1994	$96,347	$49,426	$175,387	$29,614	($94,710)	($8,524)	($73,620)
1995	$103,091	$49,426	$181,991	$29,473	($73,620)	($6,626)	($50,772)
1996	$110,308	$49,426	$188,866	$29,132	($50,772)	($4,570)	($26,210)
1997	$118,029	$49,426	$196,024	$28,569	($26,210)	($2,359)	($0)

Because the short-term borrowing rate is higher
than the rate of return from the investment of
cash surplus, the project will incur an added
interest cost of.. $6,443

(Text continued from page 141)

19, is the amount of gifts and grants required to achieve financial viability for the project under the maximum allowable tax increase—in this example, 2 mills.

Exhibits 6-20 and 6-21 present the actual and required cash-flow tables for the project. The actual cash-flow table assumes that the maximum millage rate increase of 2 mills was levied. Under this assumption, the Clayton City Park project is expected to produce a cash surplus of $153,398 over the planning period, as shown in the exhibit.

The required cash-flow table uses the 1.39 millage rate increase to calculate the project cash flows. In this case, short-term interest costs of $6,443 will be incurred as a result of the timing of the cash flows.

Supporting Calculations

If item 4 from the printing menu is selected, the model will print out a table of supporting calculations used in interim steps in producing the final solutions under each of the four funding options. The table is presented in Exhibit 6-22.

Knowledge of these data is not essential to either decision making or understanding the cash inflows and outflows from the project; however, they do provide an estimate of the expected cash flows as they will be under the inflation rates assumed by the user. This information is sometimes useful in the planning process.

Summary

The computer-assisted version of the capital budgeting model provides the user with a flexible and convenient method of working through the many calculations required to plan for the financial viability of a new capital project or noncapital program for a municipal government. In a very few minutes, the program data can be fed into the model and a set of solutions for alternative funding options can

148/CAPITAL BUDGETING FOR CITY AND COUNTY GOVERNMENTS

Exhibit 6-22: **Supporting Calculations**

				SUPPORTING CALCULATIONS						
Year	Utility Column	Inflated Construction 18.00%	Inflated Equipment 8.00%	Inflated O&M 7.00%	Inflated Non-tax 4.50%	Inflated Net Cost 9.00%	Inflated Tax Revenues PV	Gifts and Grants PV	Gifts and Grants Distribution	Distribution PV
	(a)	(b)	(c)	(d)	(e)	(f)	(g)	(h)	(i)	(j)
Current:										
1987										
Project:										
1988	$0	$250,000	$0	$0	$0	$229,358	$60,550	$348,624	63.3%	0.58104
1989	$0	$350,000	$0	$0	$0	$294,588	$56,662	$92,585	18.3%	0.15431
1990	$0	$400,000	$188,957	$0	$0	$454,783	$53,023	$69,497	15.0%	0.11583
1991	$91,000	$0	$0	$78,648	$108,519	($21,162)	$49,618	$14,169	3.3%	0.02361
1992	$91,000	$0	$0	$84,153	$113,403	($19,010)	$46,431	$0	0.0%	0.00000
1993	$91,000	$0	$0	$90,044	$118,506	($16,971)	$43,450	$0	0.0%	0.00000
1994	$91,000	$0	$0	$96,347	$123,838	($15,039)	$40,659	$0	0.0%	0.00000
1995	$91,000	$0	$0	$103,091	$129,411	($13,209)	$38,048	$0	0.0%	0.00000
1996	$91,000	$0	$0	$110,308	$135,235	($11,477)	$35,605	$0	0.0%	0.00000
1997	$91,000	$0	$0	$118,029	$141,320	($9,838)	$33,318	$0	0.0%	0.00000
Totals	$637,000	$1,000,000	$188,957	$680,619	$870,232	$872,022	$457,365	$524,874	100.0%	0.87479

be computed and analyzed. Moreover, the basic planning parameters easily can be changed to test alternative sets of assumptions regarding interest rates, inflation rates, fund-raising activities, and borrowing arrangements. Significant amounts of time can therefore be saved through the application of the computer-assisted model. But more important, the convenience of the model will permit a much more extensive analysis of each of the projects being analyzed, thereby improving the municipality's overall capital budgeting process.

Endnote

1. Lotus 1-2-3 is a registered trademark of Lotus Development Corporation. The Lotus 1-2-3 template, developed by Sheila Frazier, may be obtained from the publisher. The user should become familiar with the operation of the Lotus 1-2-3 software before he or she attempts to use this template. Instructions for the use of Lotus are not provided in this book.